Suzi Spirit Sensitive's

Meditation Journal

This Meditation Journal belongs to

____

The Energy Tree
Life Coaching - Spiritual Guidance

Meditation Journal
Design by Craftypads.
ISBN: 9781693523397
Imprint: Independently published by The Energy Tree

email: theenergytree@gmail.com

Welcome to your Meditation Journal. This book is designed to help you analyse and record all methods you use for meditation plus everything you see, hear, feel and smell in your meditation.

This is an amazing technique for relaxing and highering your vibration. If you are new to meditation, be patient with yourself. It takes time to quiet the mind enough in order to have that etheral experience where you can connect to energies all around you or sit in your own power. It is as simple as finding a quiet space where you will not be interrupted and either sitting in silence while breathing deep or listening to some music that helps relax you. There are many guided and non-guided meditation videos on YouTube available for free.

As you delve into this world of connection and relaxation, you will come into a space where you are aware yet not aware of yourself and everything around you. It is the most wonderful experience and you can even use meditation to communicate with Spirit Guides and loved ones who have passed on into the Spirit World. You can also use meditation to ground yourself and find clarity in a hectic situation.

So dive right into a multitude of experiences available to you through simple meditation. Be patient and absorb every message that is sent to you from your Higher Self and those in the Spirit World or just enjoy the relaxation that will wash over you each and every time you allow yourself to let go of tension and stress.

Love and light to you and may this book bring you peace and enlightenment.

How to use this book.

This journal is for you to record and analyse your experiences in meditation. By recording what you do to sink into a meditative state and by writing down or drawing what you see, feel, hear and smell, you can look back and decipher messages that may be passed to you from the spirit world. You can use your reflection space to interpret what you think certain elements of your meditation mean for you and also to record how you felt before meditating versus how you feel after.

At the back of this book is space for you to compile your meditation playlists. What music sends you into that trance state? Write it all down and note changes in your methods particularly if they make your go into a deeper state of trance or give you clearer messages.

Record and analyse and watch the beauty unfold as you experience the ultimate communication with spirit and the best relaxation method in the world.

What are you meditating to?

How do you feel before meditation?

What did you smell?

What did you hear?

What did you see?

Reflection.

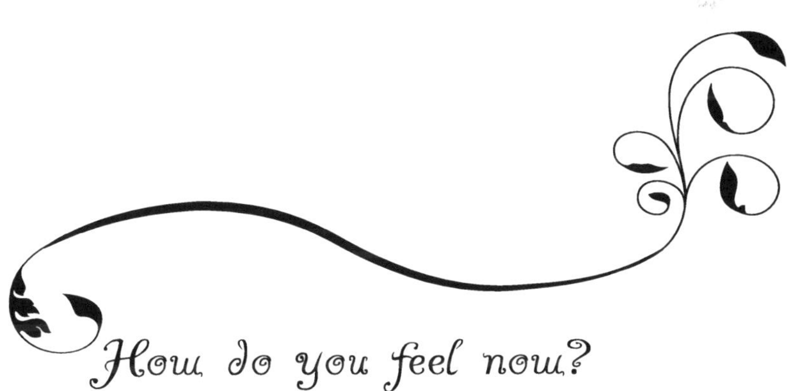

How do you feel now?

Date

__/____/____

What are you meditating to?

How do you feel before meditation?

What did you smell?

What did you hear?

What did you see?

Reflection.

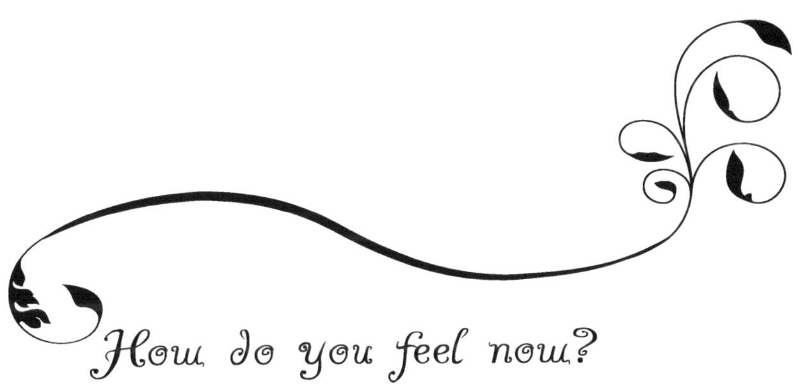

How do you feel now?

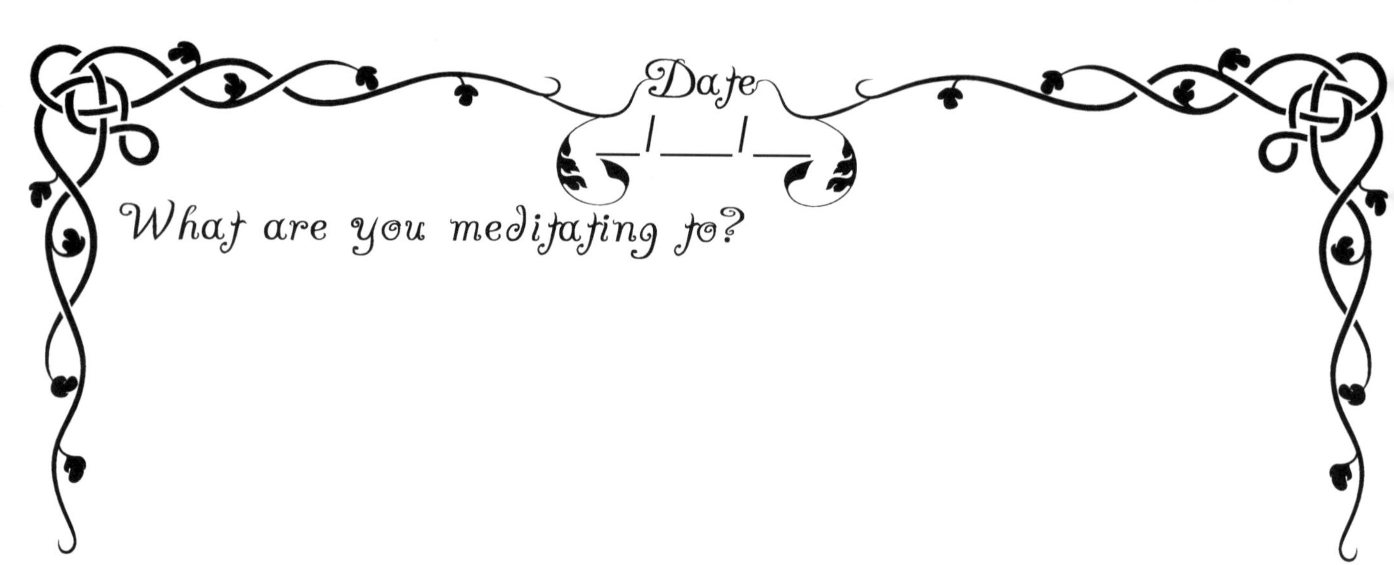

Date

__/____/___

What are you meditating to?

How do you feel before meditation?

What did you smell?

What did you hear?

What did you see?

Reflection.

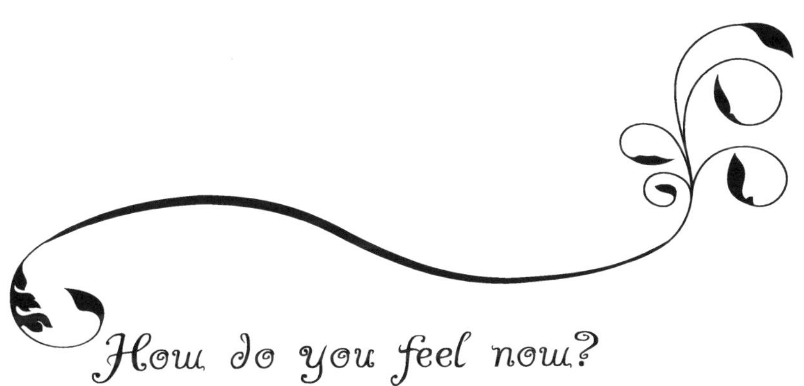

How do you feel now?

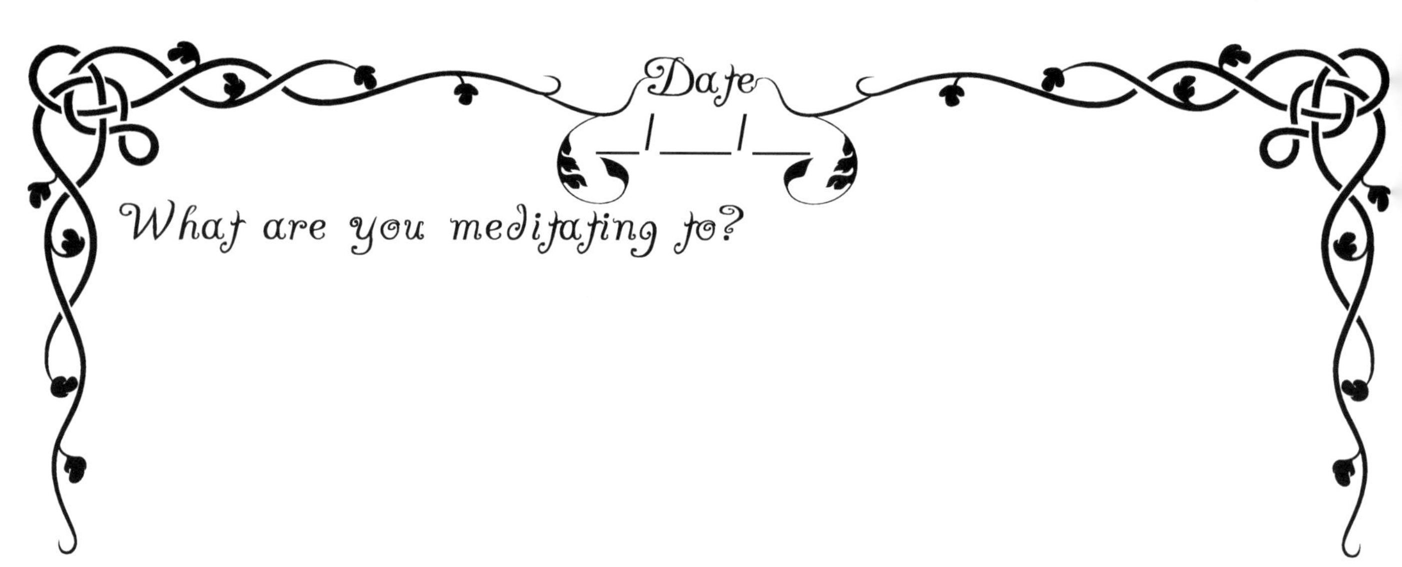

Date

__/__/__

What are you meditating to?

How do you feel before meditation?

What did you smell?

What did you hear?

What did you see?

Reflection.

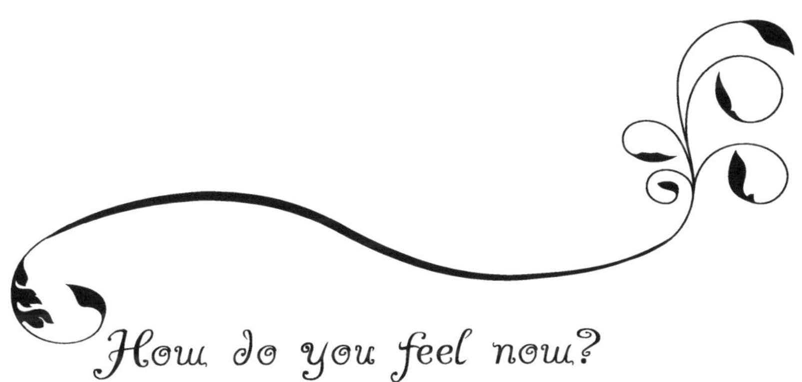

How do you feel now?

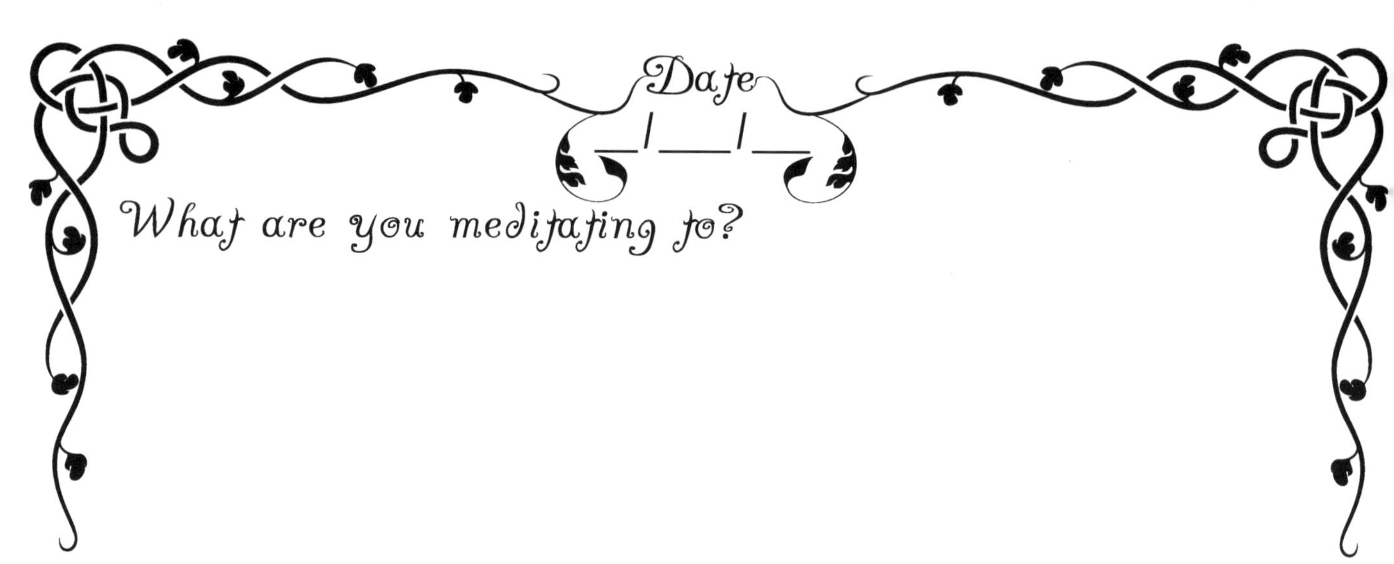

Date
__/__/__

What are you meditating to?

How do you feel before meditation?

What did you smell?

What did you hear?

What did you see?

Reflection.

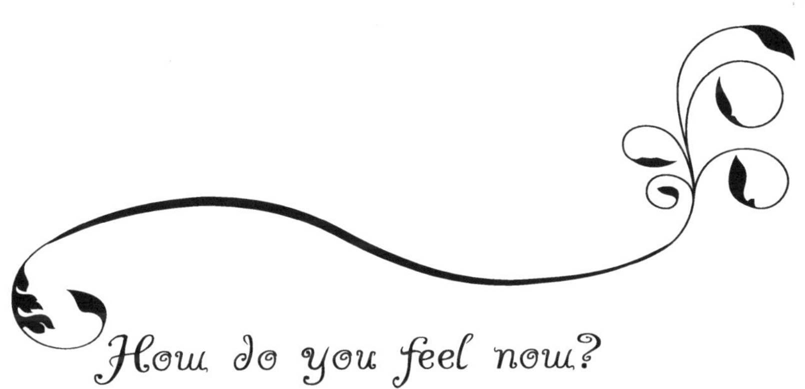

How do you feel now?

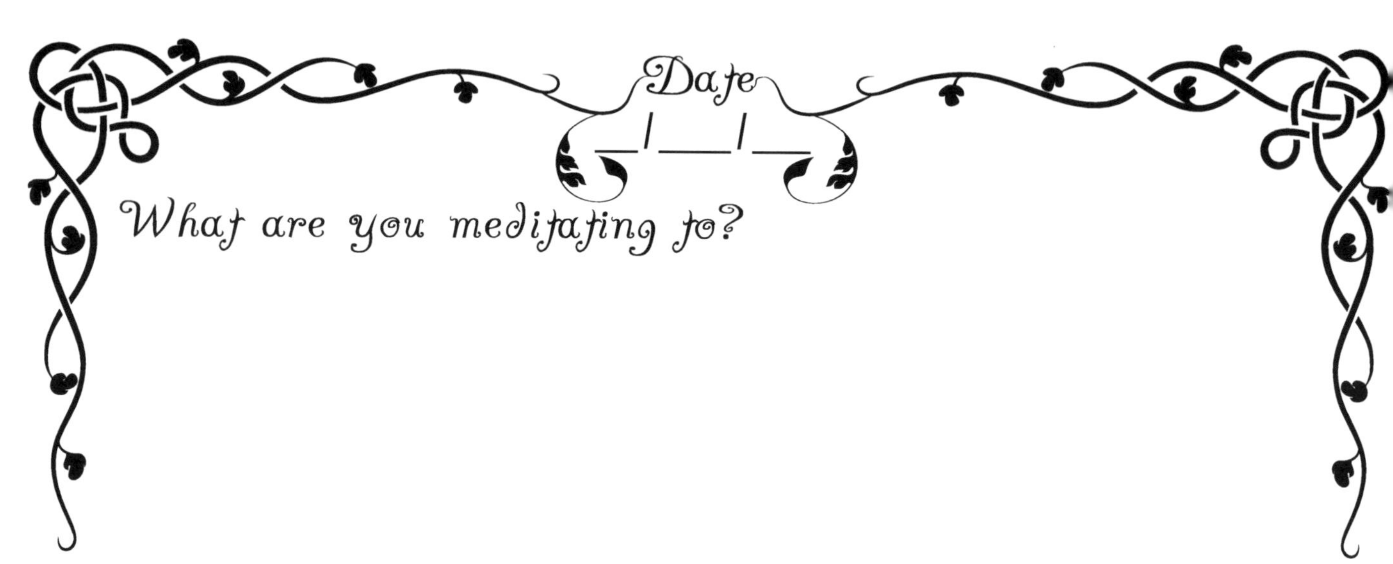

Date

__/__/__

What are you meditating to?

How do you feel before meditation?

What did you smell?

What did you hear?

What did you see?

Reflection.

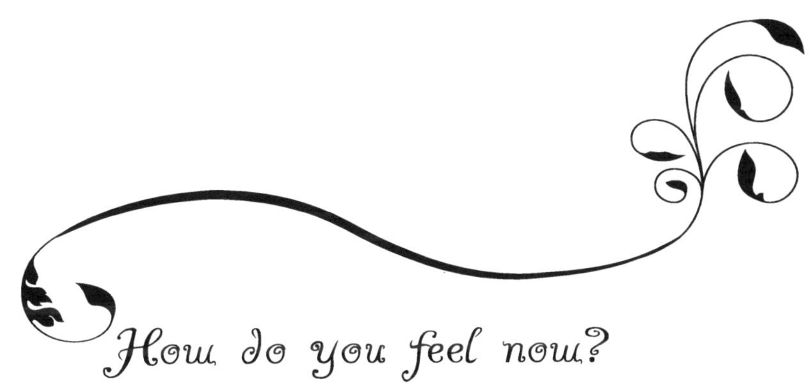

How do you feel now?

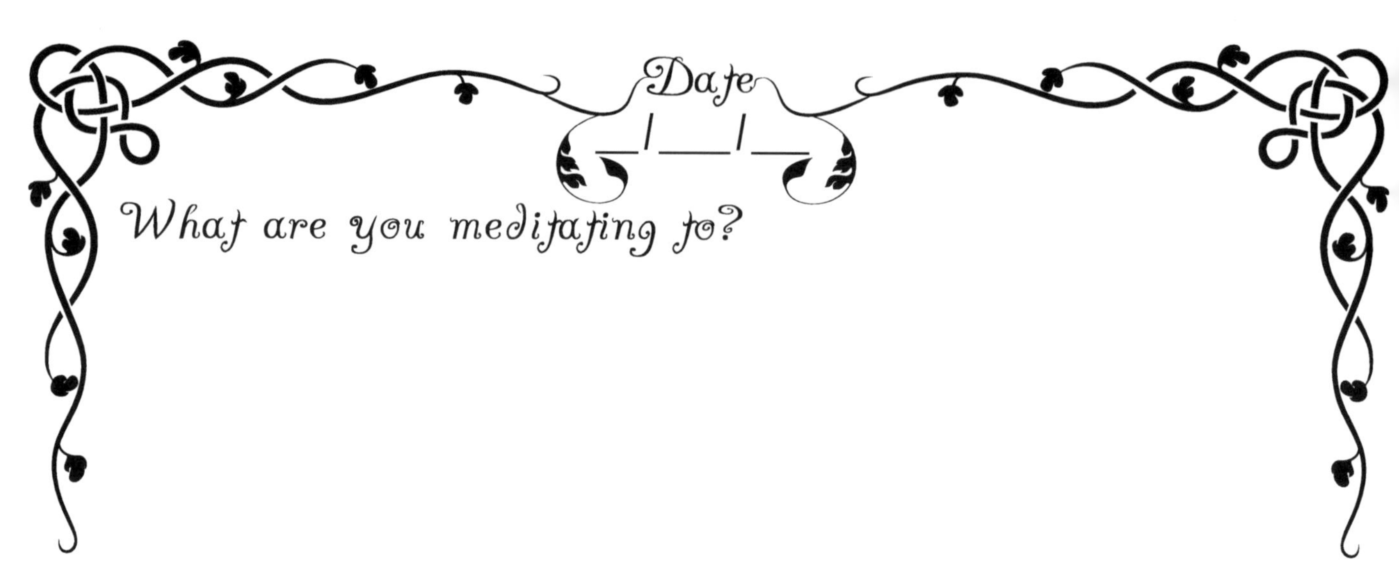

Date

__/__/__

What are you meditating to?

How do you feel before meditation?

What did you smell?

What did you hear?

What did you see?

Reflection.

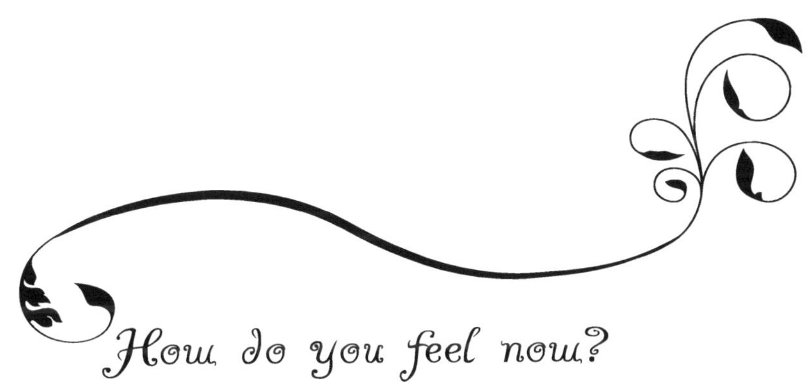

How do you feel now?

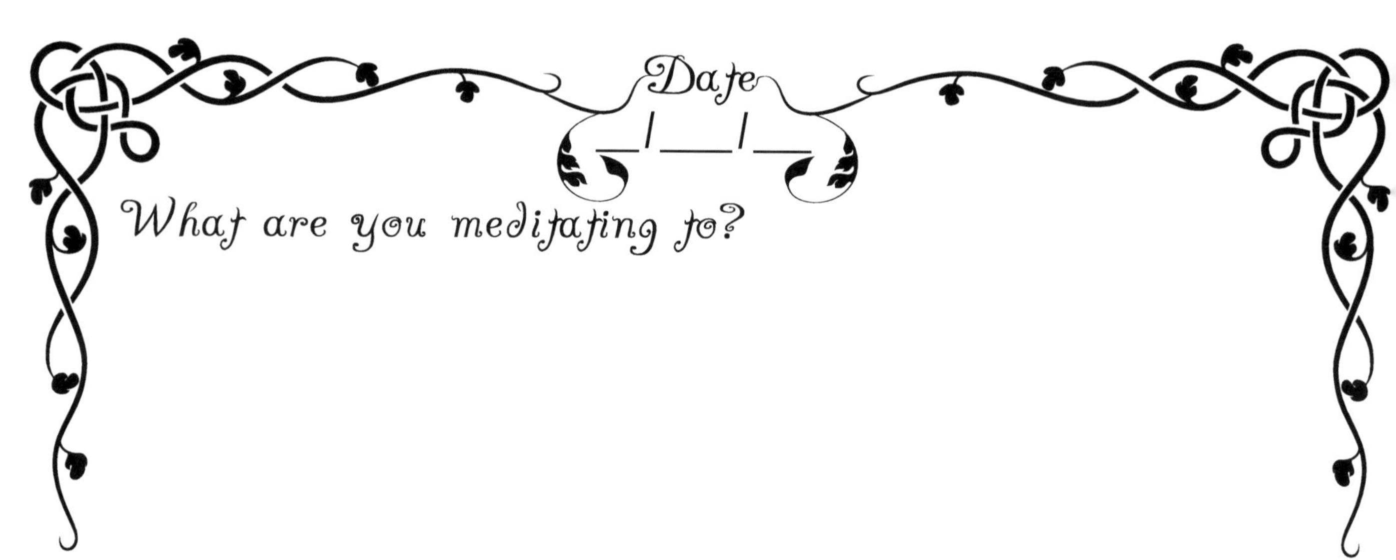

Date
__/__/__

What are you meditating to?

How do you feel before meditation?

What did you smell?

What did you hear?

What did you see?

Reflection.

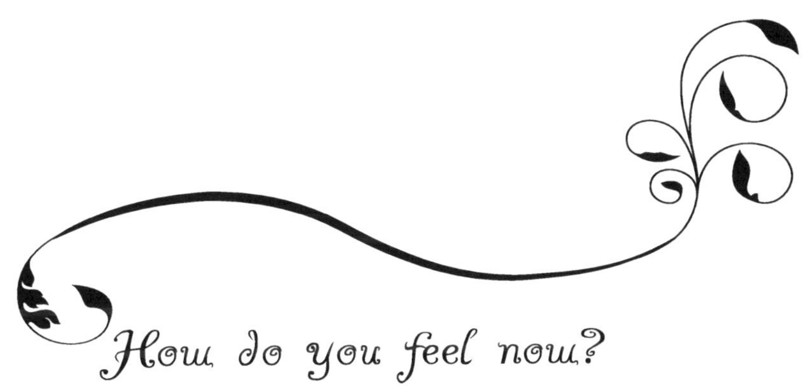

How do you feel now?

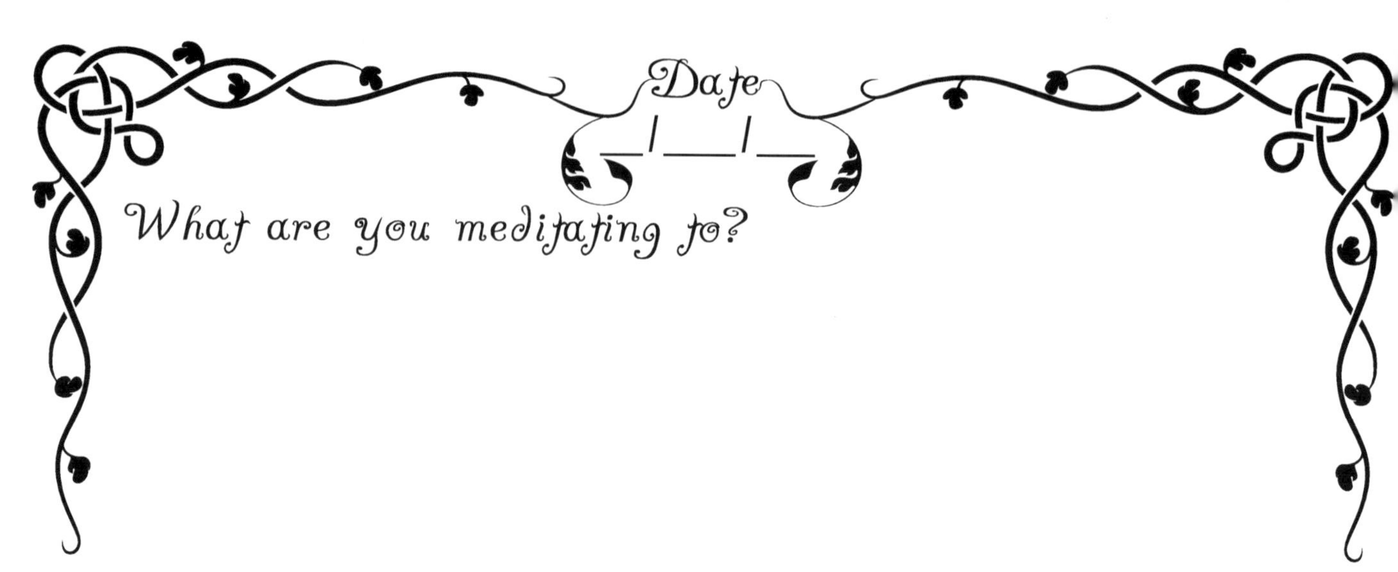

What are you meditating to?

How do you feel before meditation?

What did you smell?

What did you hear?

What did you see?

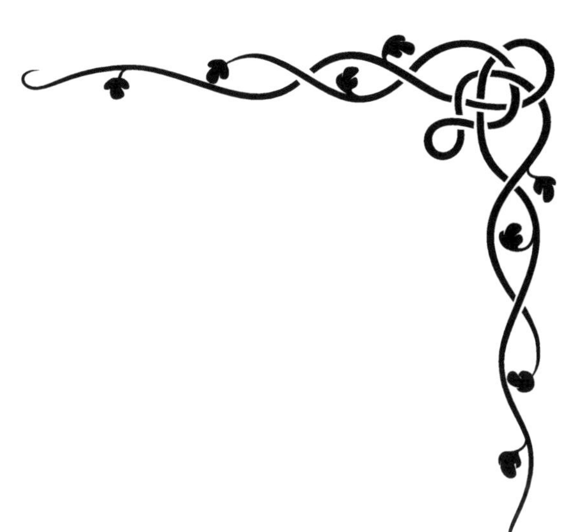

Reflection.

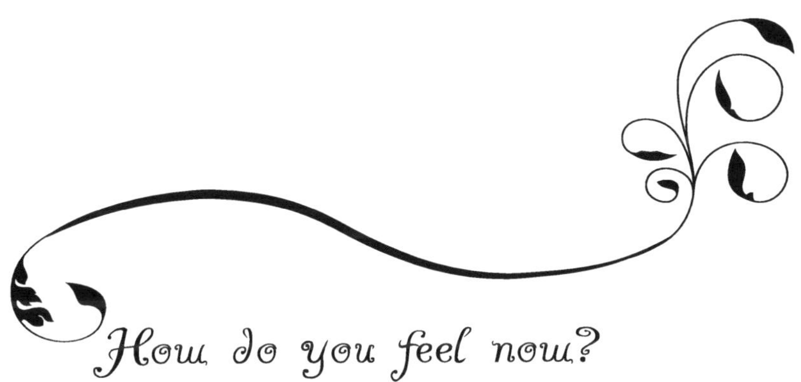

How do you feel now?

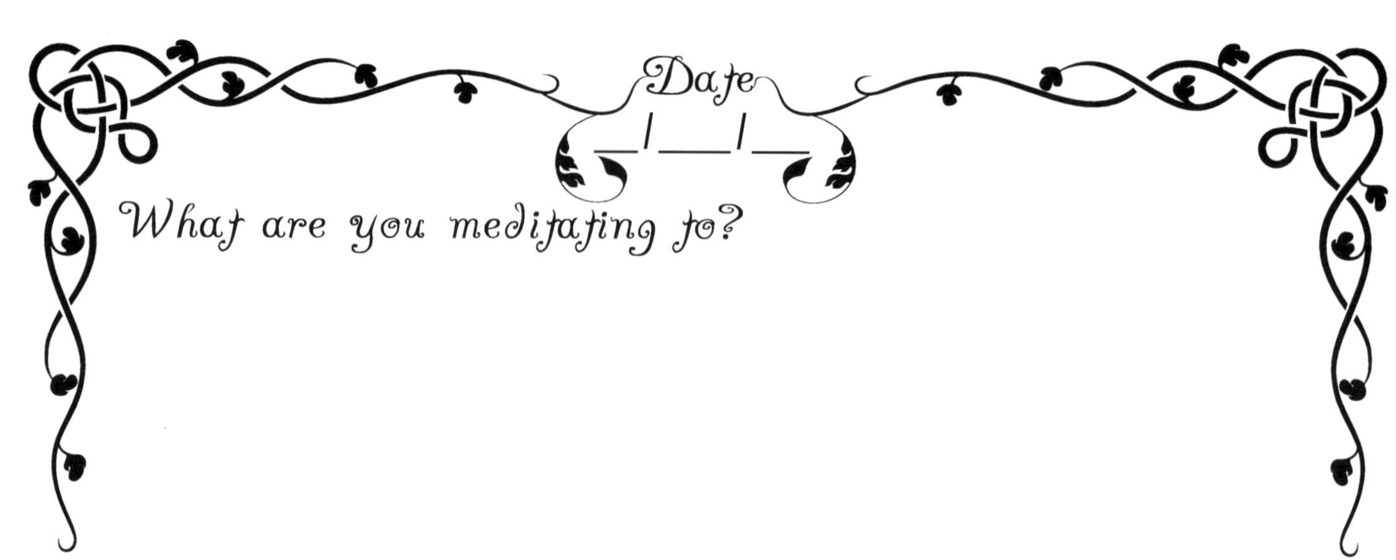

Date
__/__/__

What are you meditating to?

How do you feel before meditation?

What did you smell?

What did you hear?

What did you see?

Reflection.

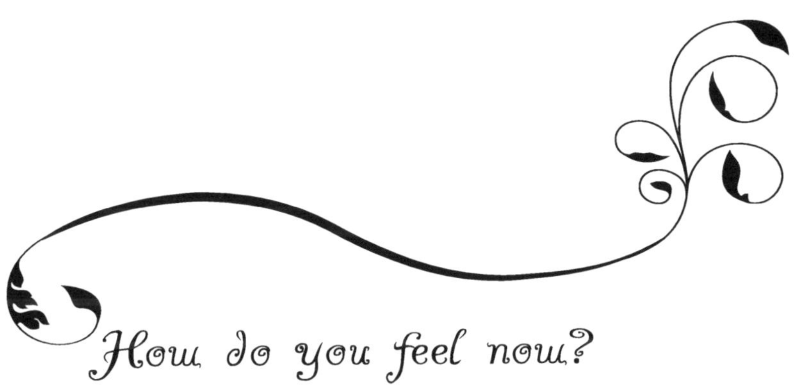

How do you feel now?

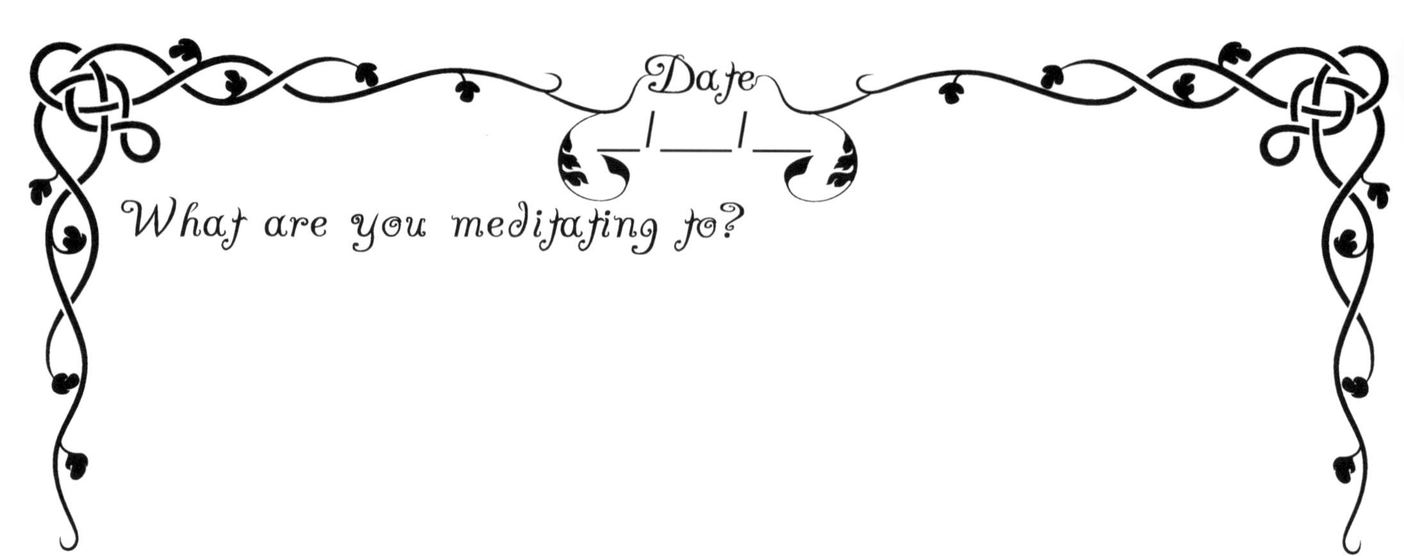

Date

__/__/__

What are you meditating to?

How do you feel before meditation?

What did you smell?

What did you hear?

What did you see?

Reflection.

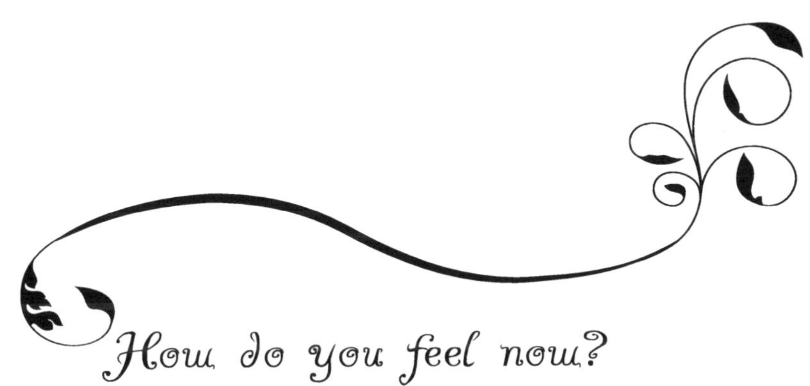

How do you feel now?

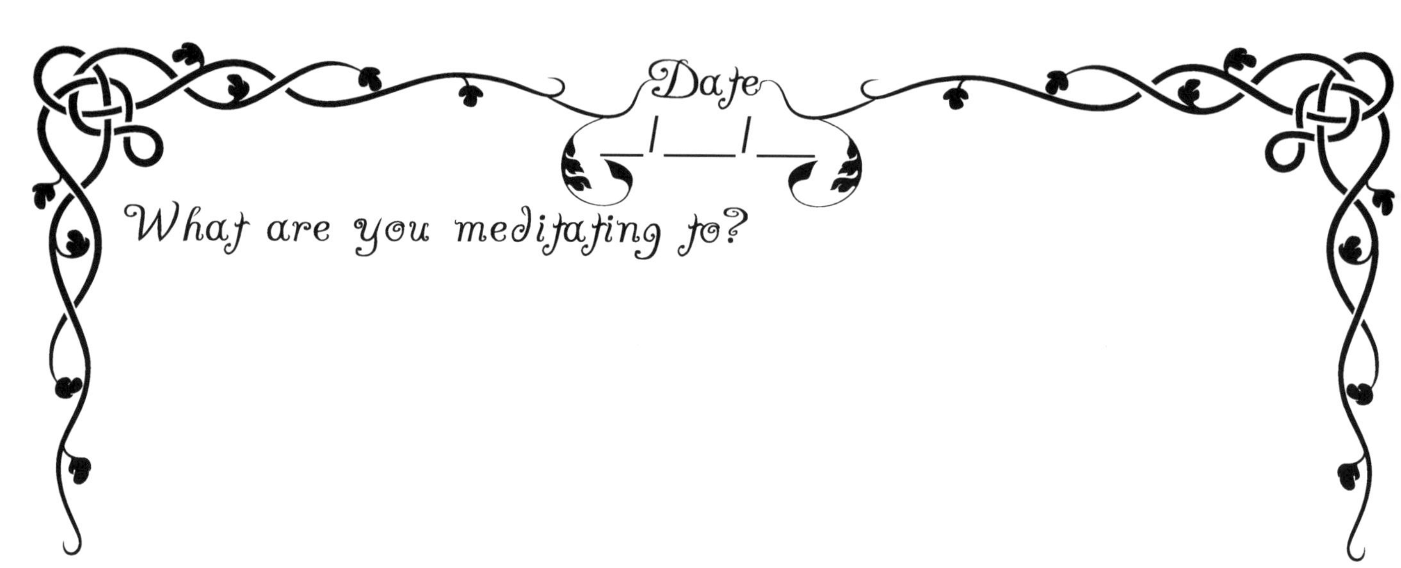

Date

__/__/__

What are you meditating to?

How do you feel before meditation?

What did you smell?

What did you hear?

What did you see?

Reflection.

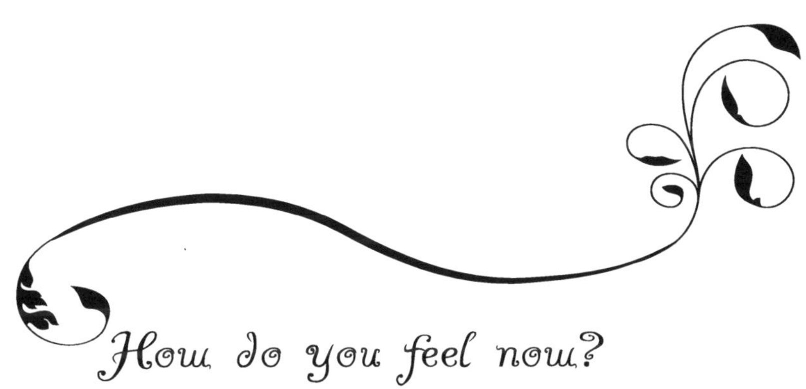

How do you feel now?

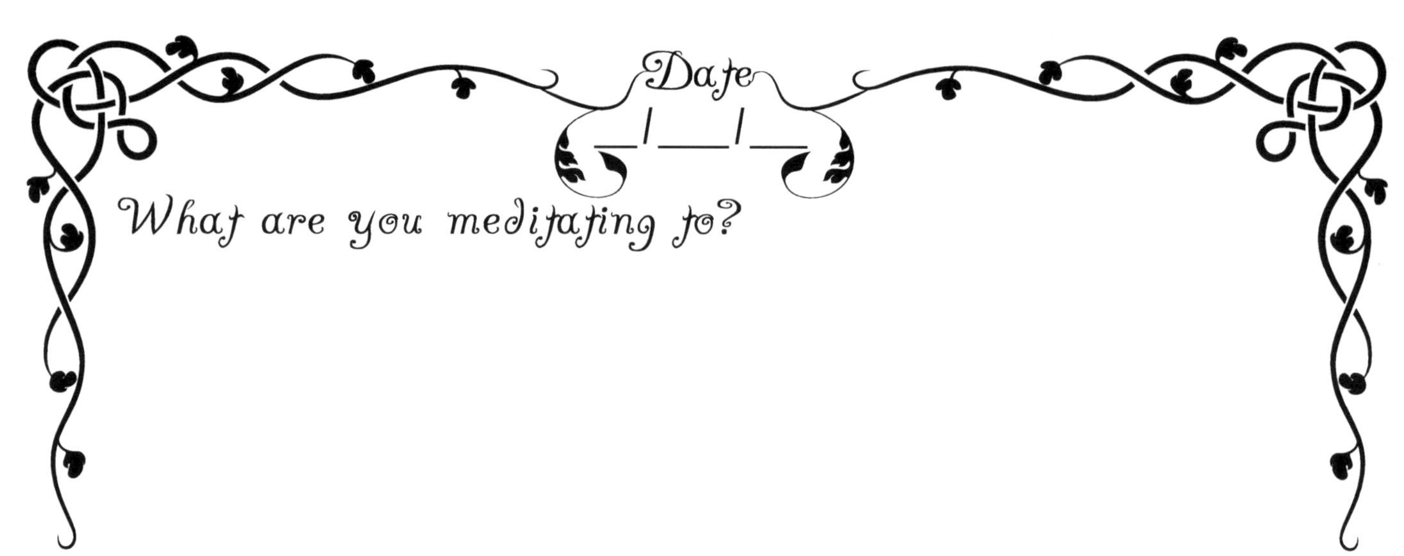

Date
__/__/__

What are you meditating to?

How do you feel before meditation?

What did you smell?

What did you hear?

What did you see?

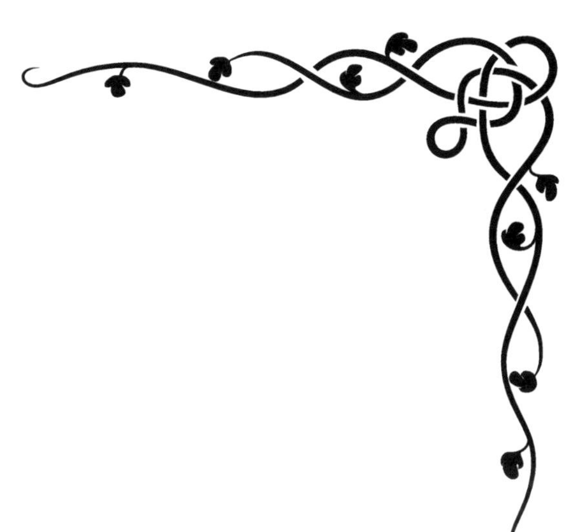

Reflection.

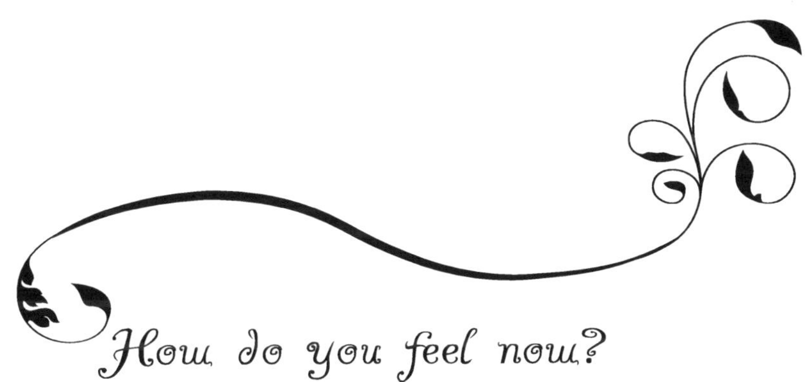

How do you feel now?

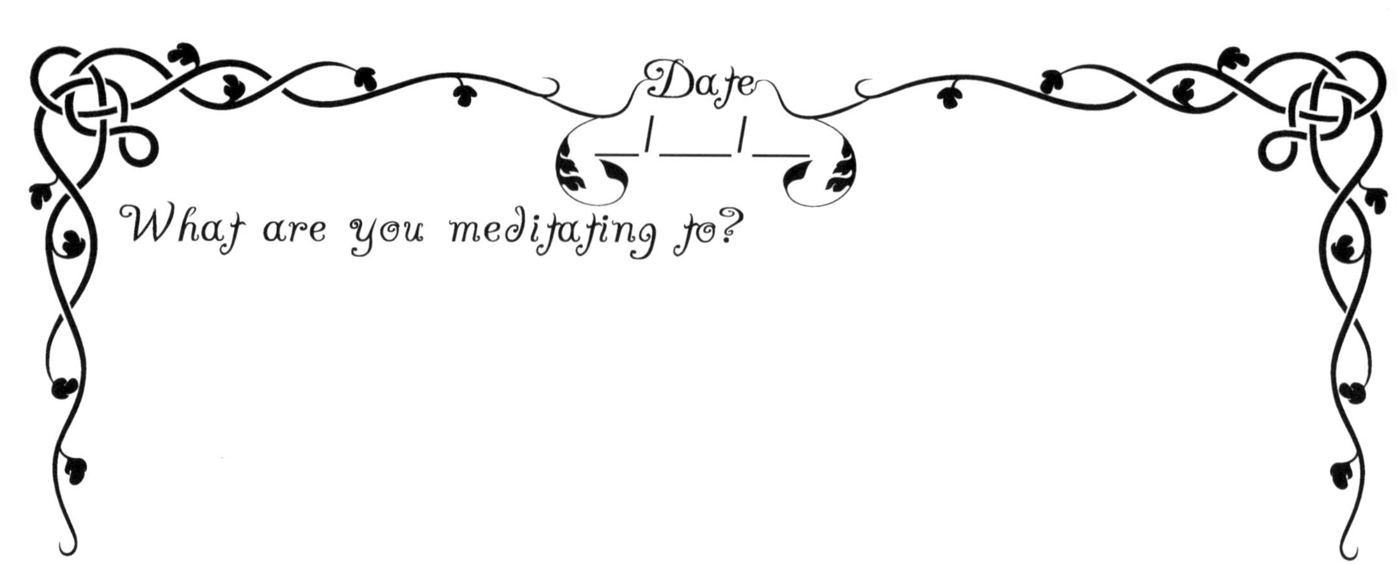

Date
__/__/__

What are you meditating to?

How do you feel before meditation?

What did you smell?

What did you hear?

What did you see?

Reflection.

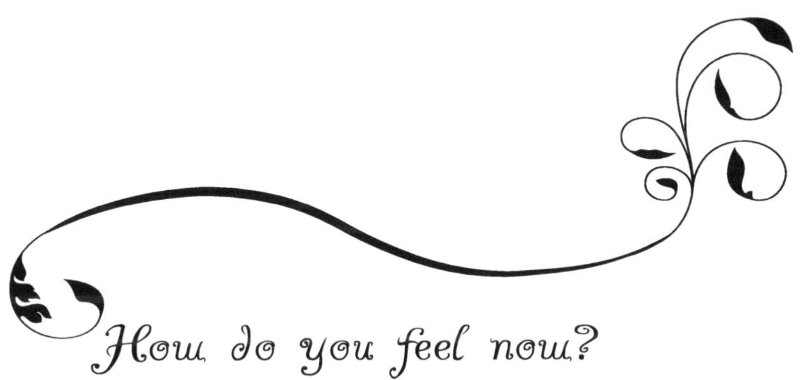

How do you feel now?

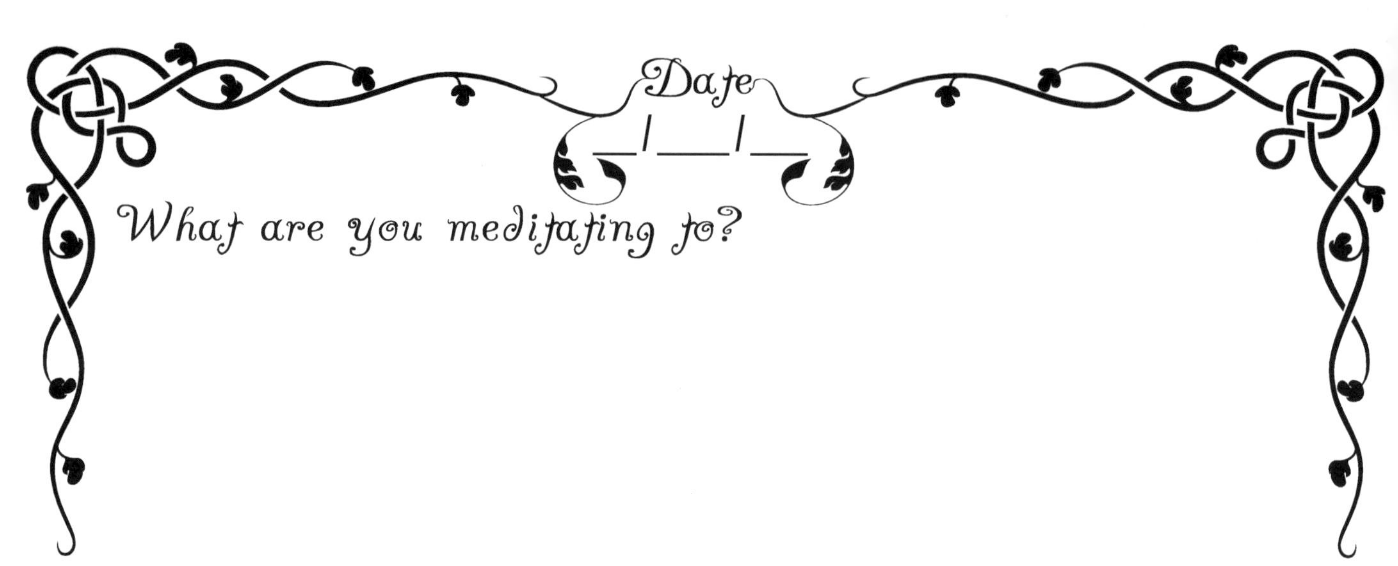

What are you meditating to?

How do you feel before meditation?

What did you smell?

What did you hear?

What did you see?

Reflection.

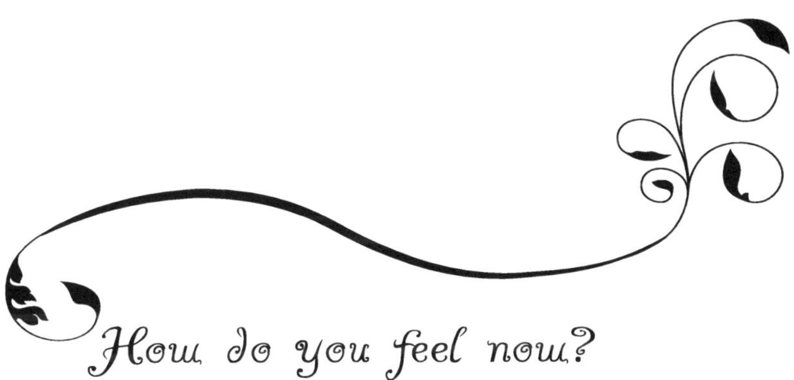

How do you feel now?

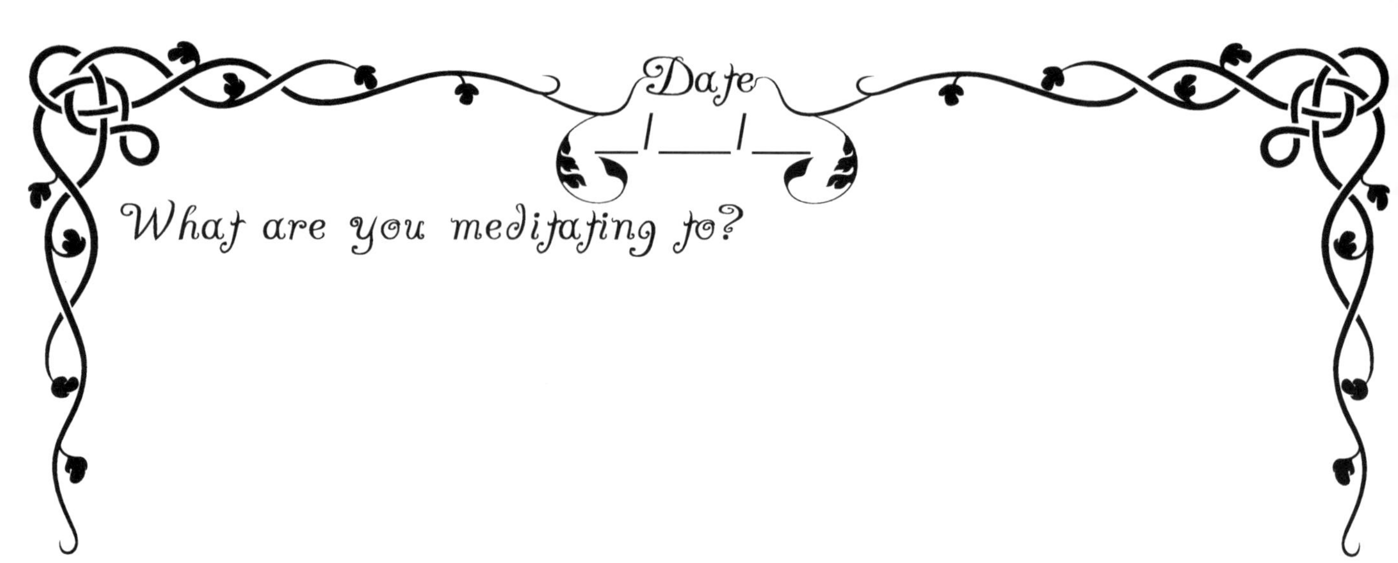

Date

__/__/__

What are you meditating to?

How do you feel before meditation?

What did you smell?

What did you hear?

What did you see?

Reflection.

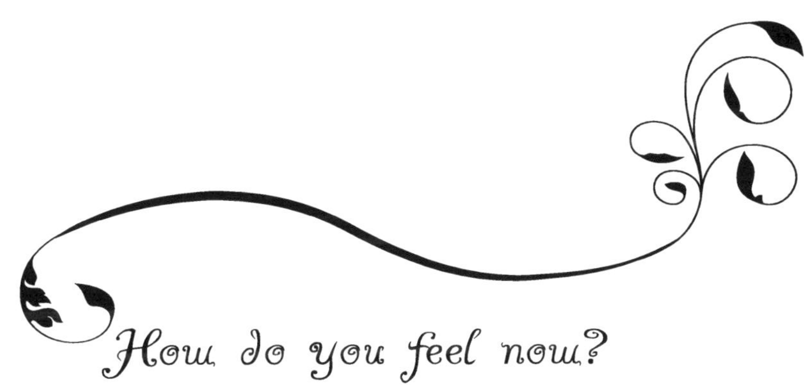

How do you feel now?

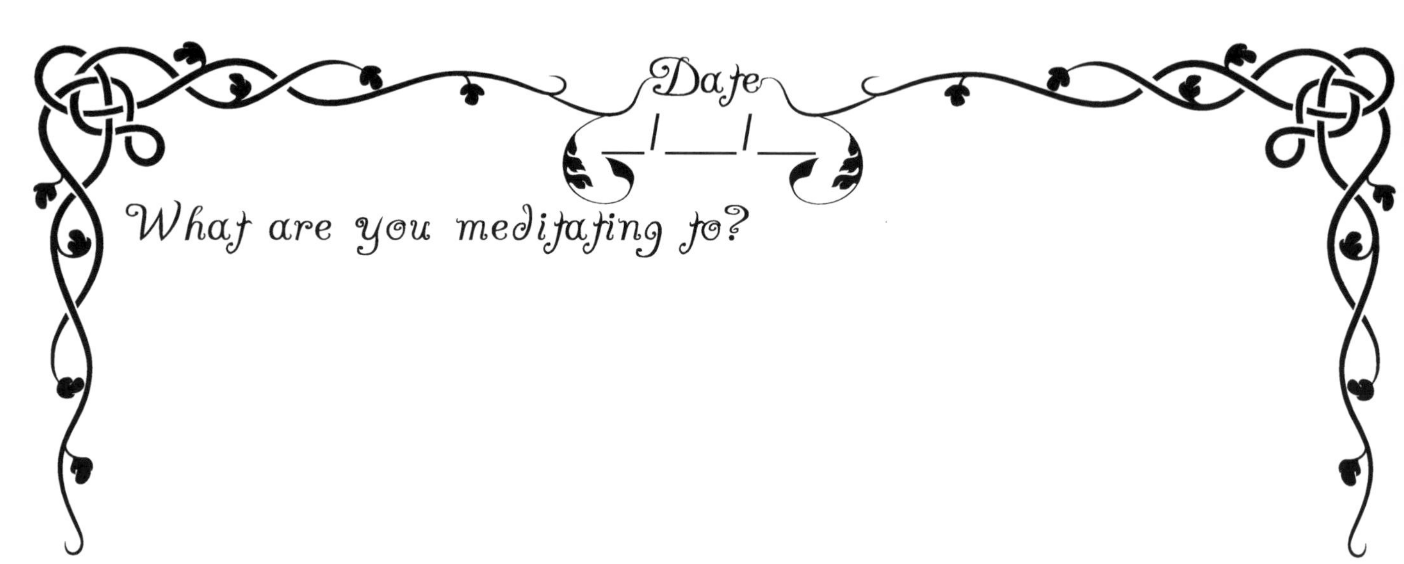

Date
__/__/__

What are you meditating to?

How do you feel before meditation?

What did you smell?

What did you hear?

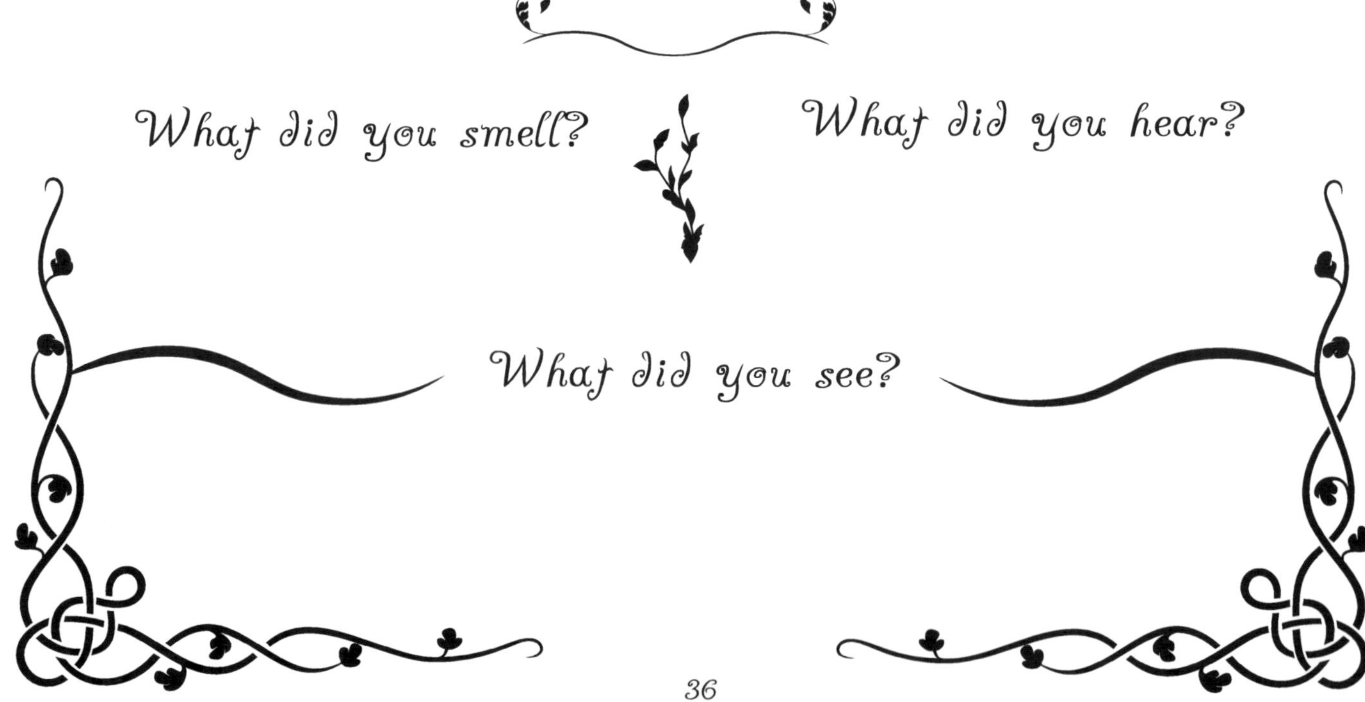

What did you see?

Reflection.

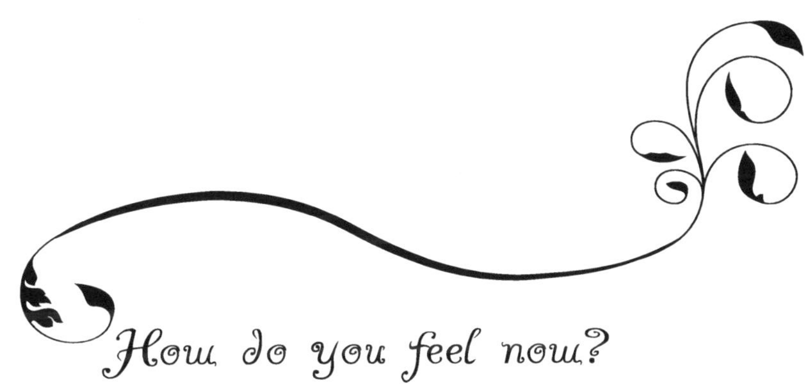

How do you feel now?

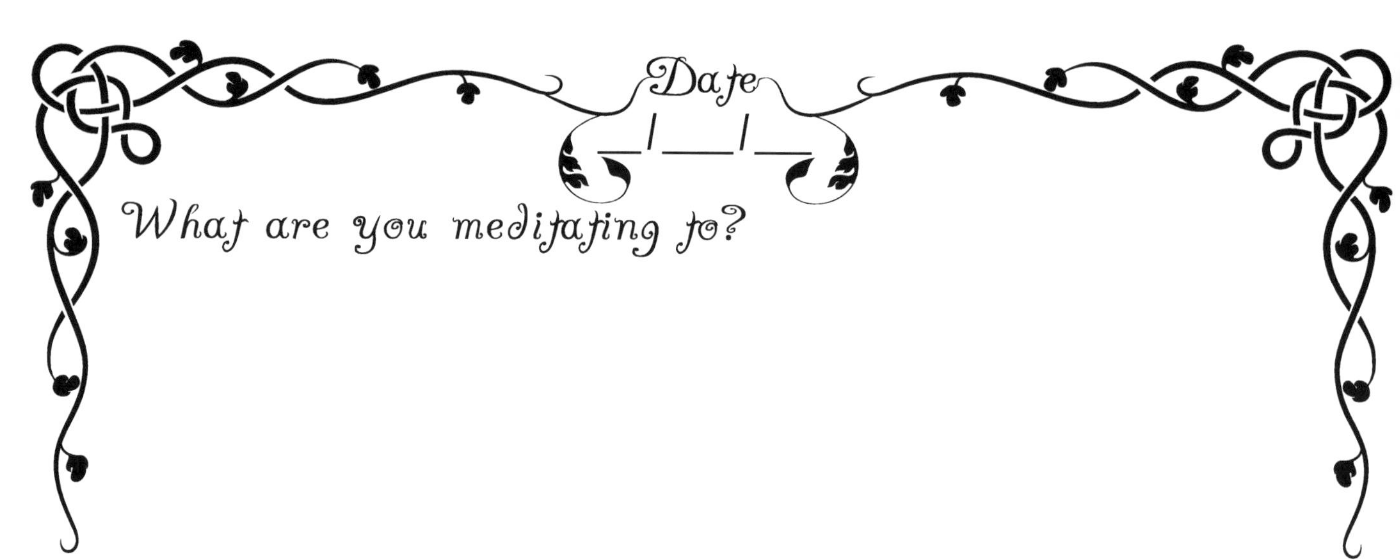

Date

__/__/__

What are you meditating to?

How do you feel before meditation?

What did you smell?

What did you hear?

What did you see?

Reflection.

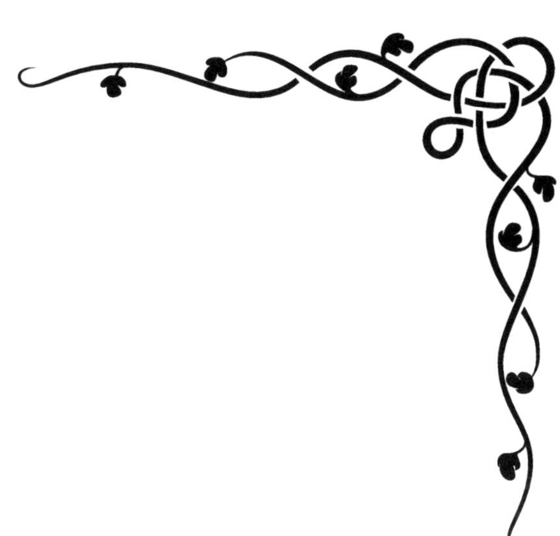

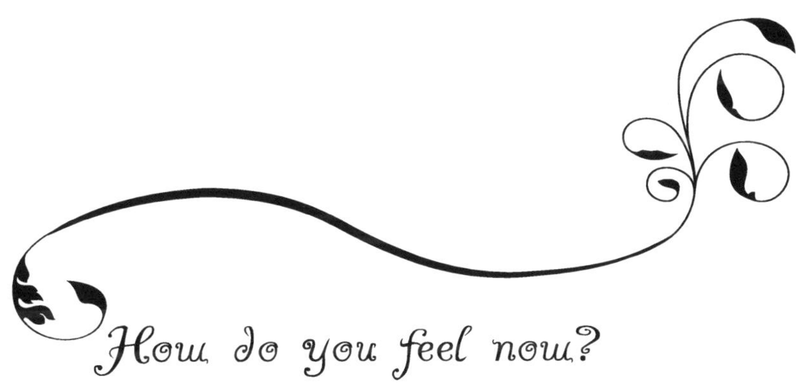

How do you feel now?

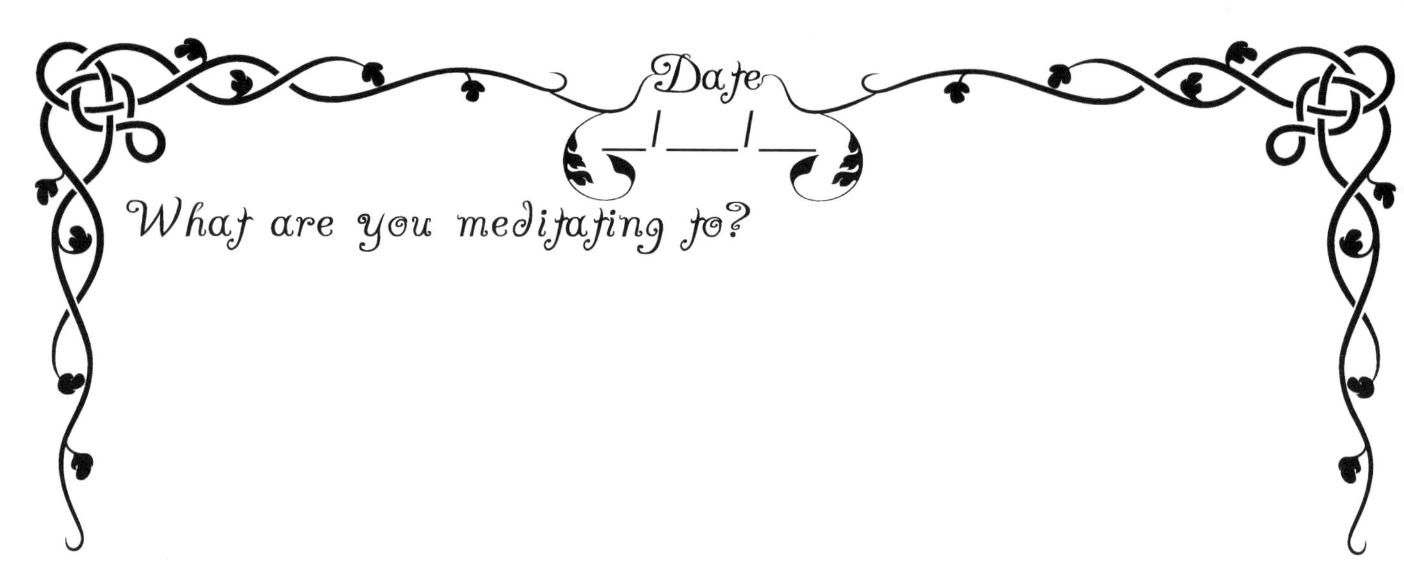

Date

__/__/__

What are you meditating to?

How do you feel before meditation?

What did you smell?

What did you hear?

What did you see?

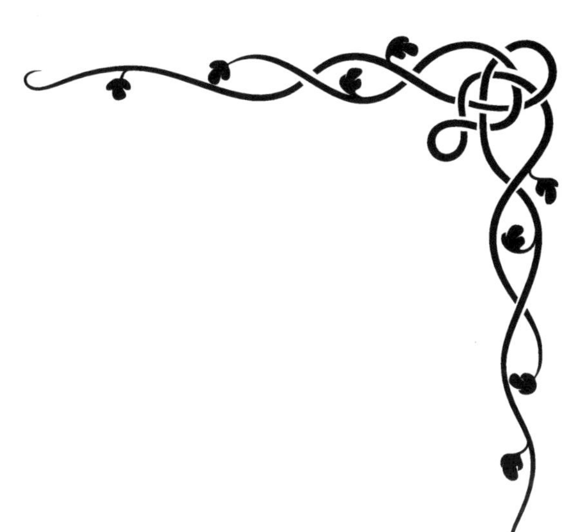

Reflection.

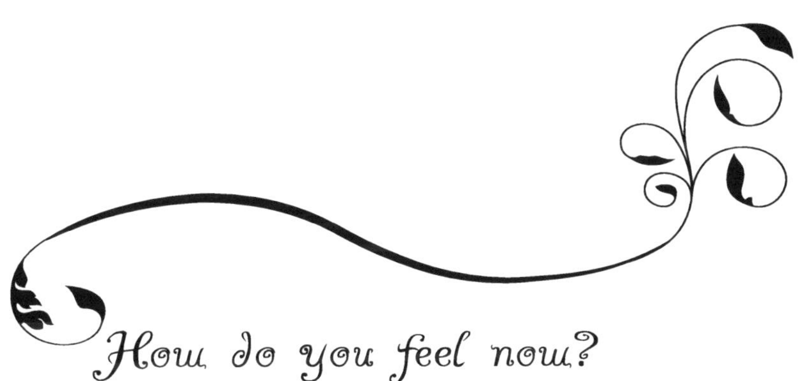

How do you feel now?

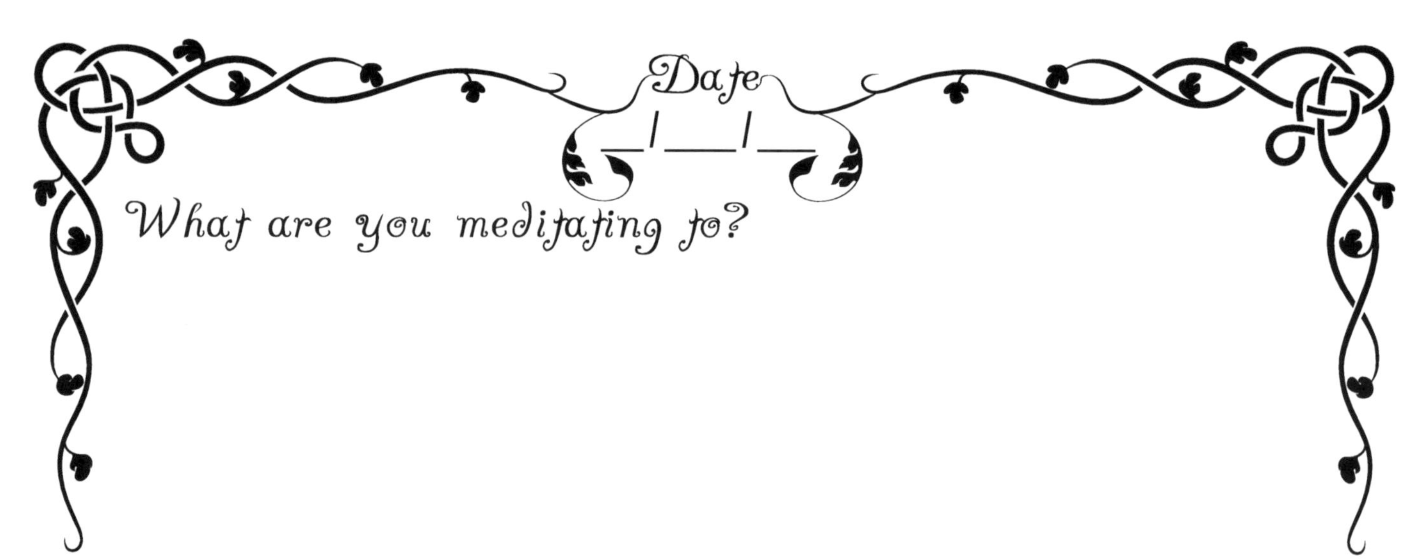

Date

__/__/__

What are you meditating to?

How do you feel before meditation?

What did you smell?

What did you hear?

What did you see?

Reflection.

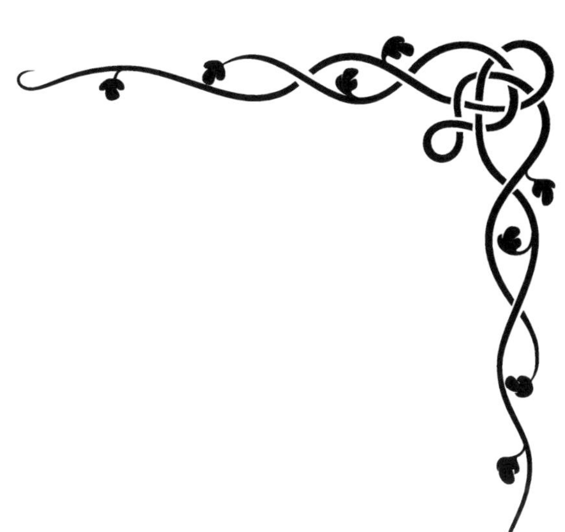

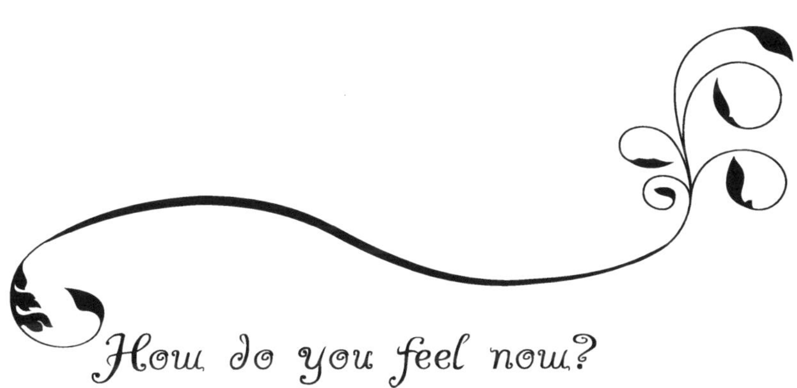

How do you feel now?

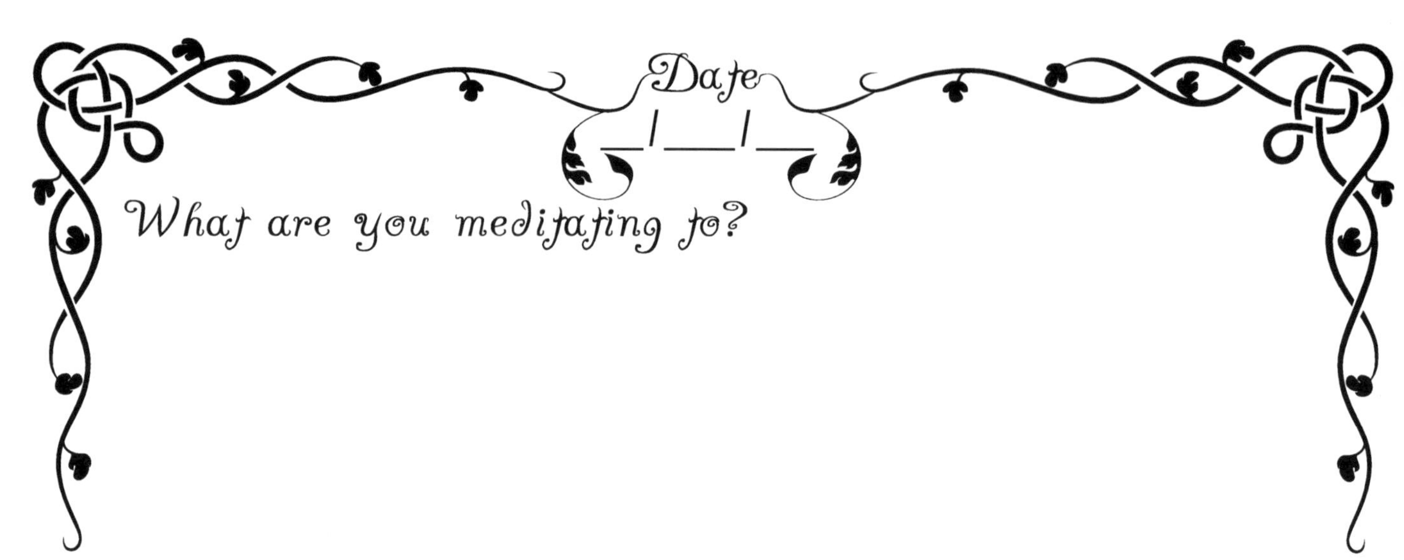

Date
__/__/__

What are you meditating to?

How do you feel before meditation?

What did you smell?

What did you hear?

What did you see?

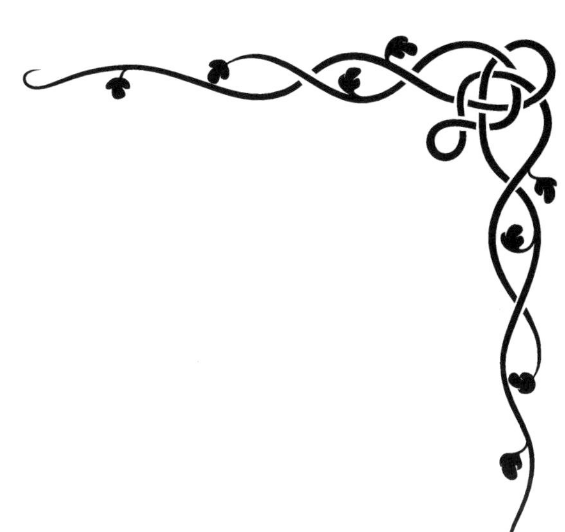

Reflection.

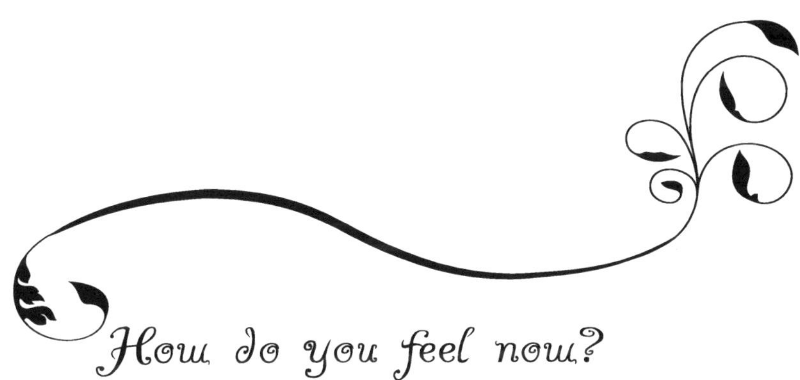

How do you feel now?

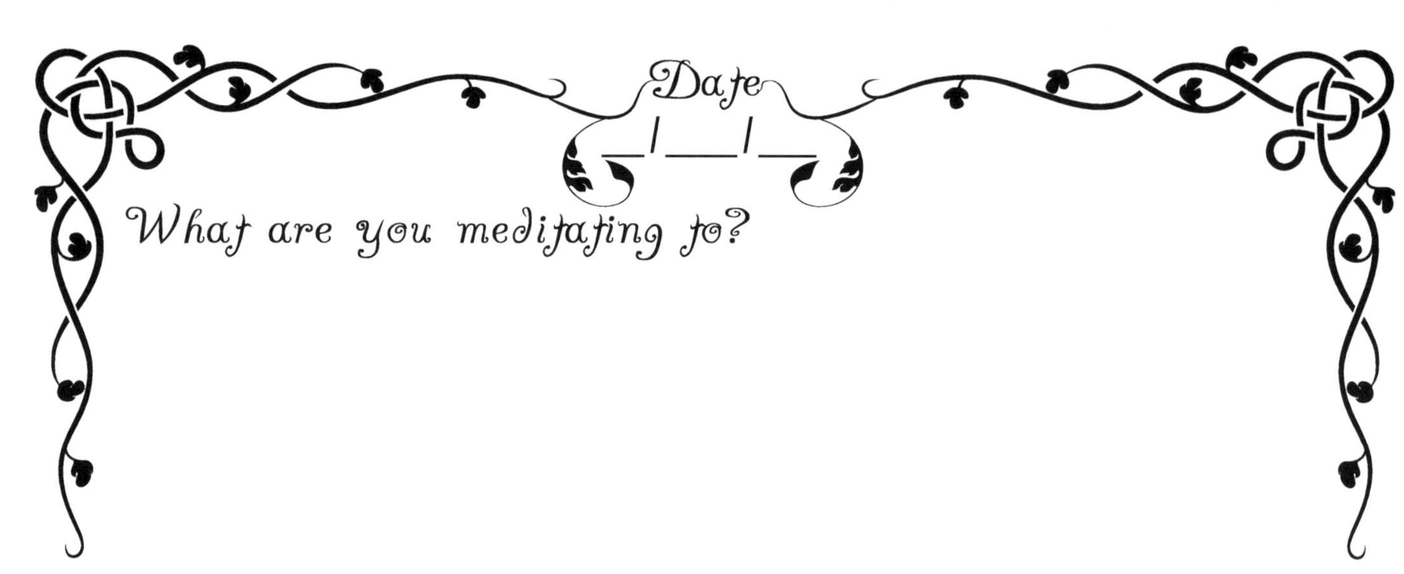

Date

__/__/__

What are you meditating to?

How do you feel before meditation?

What did you smell?

What did you hear?

What did you see?

Reflection.

How do you feel now?

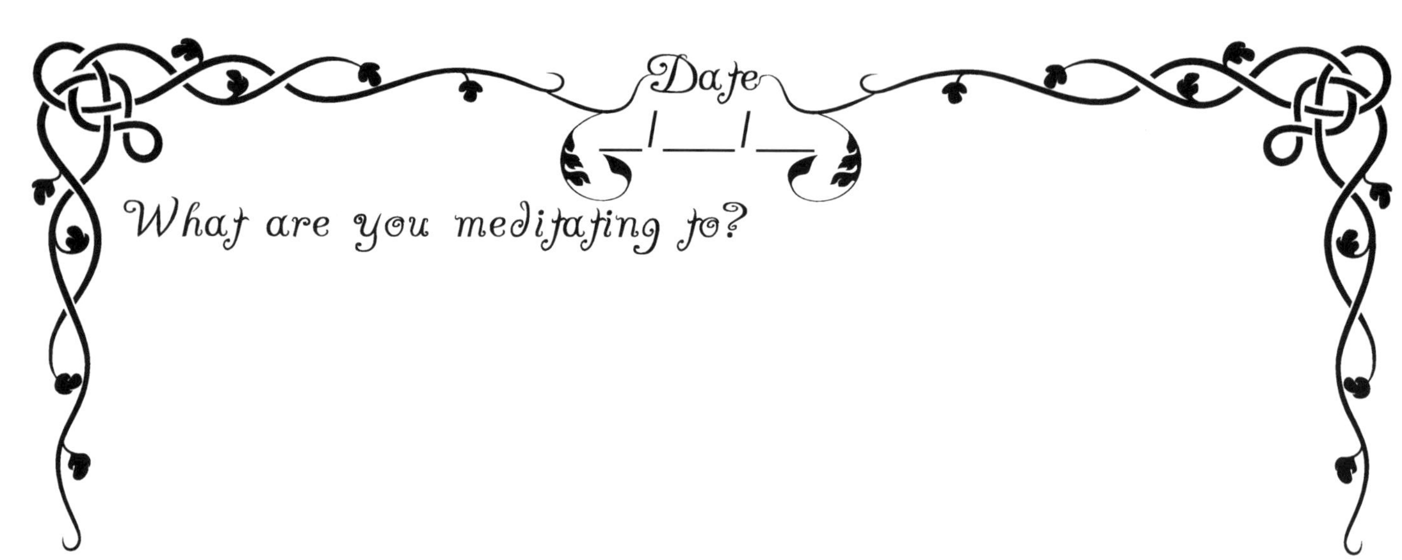

What are you meditating to?

How do you feel before meditation?

What did you smell?

What did you hear?

What did you see?

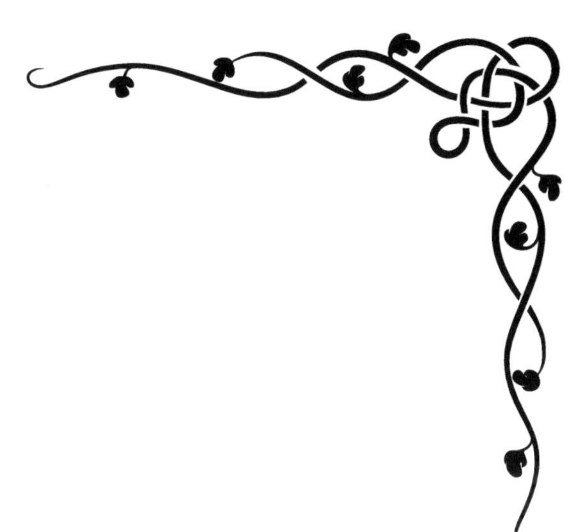

Reflection.

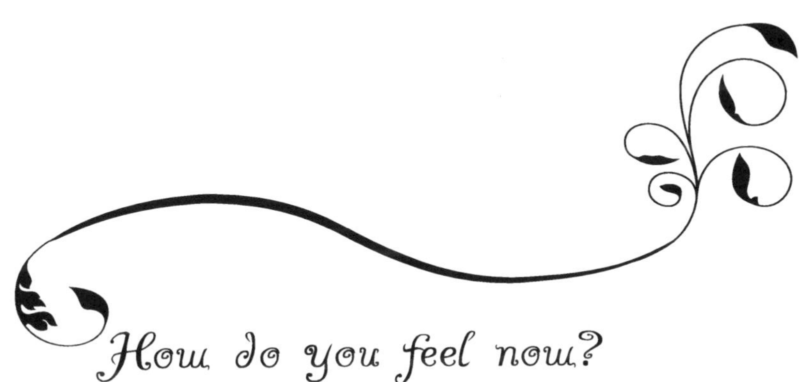

How do you feel now?

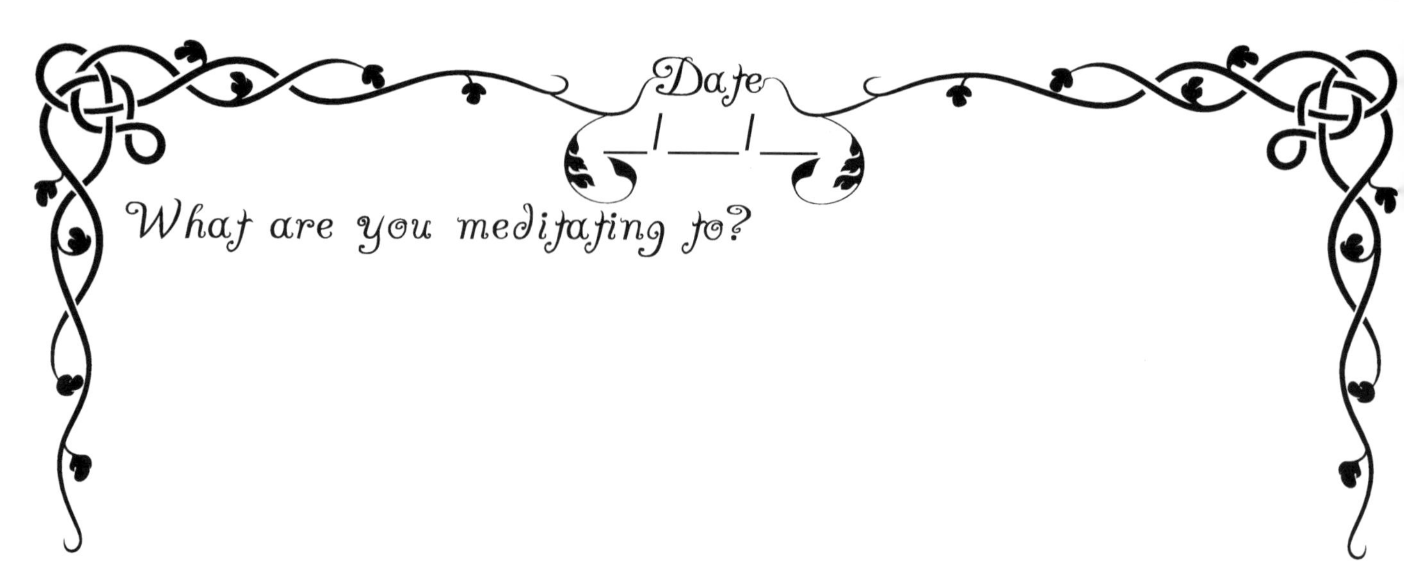

Date

__/__/__

What are you meditating to?

How do you feel before meditation?

What did you smell?

What did you hear?

What did you see?

Reflection.

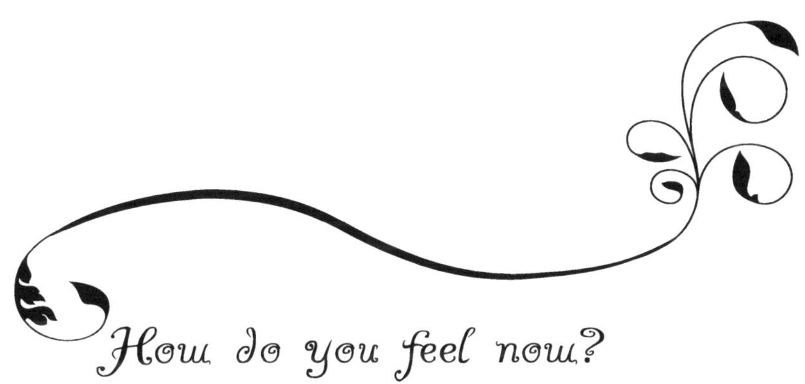

How do you feel now?

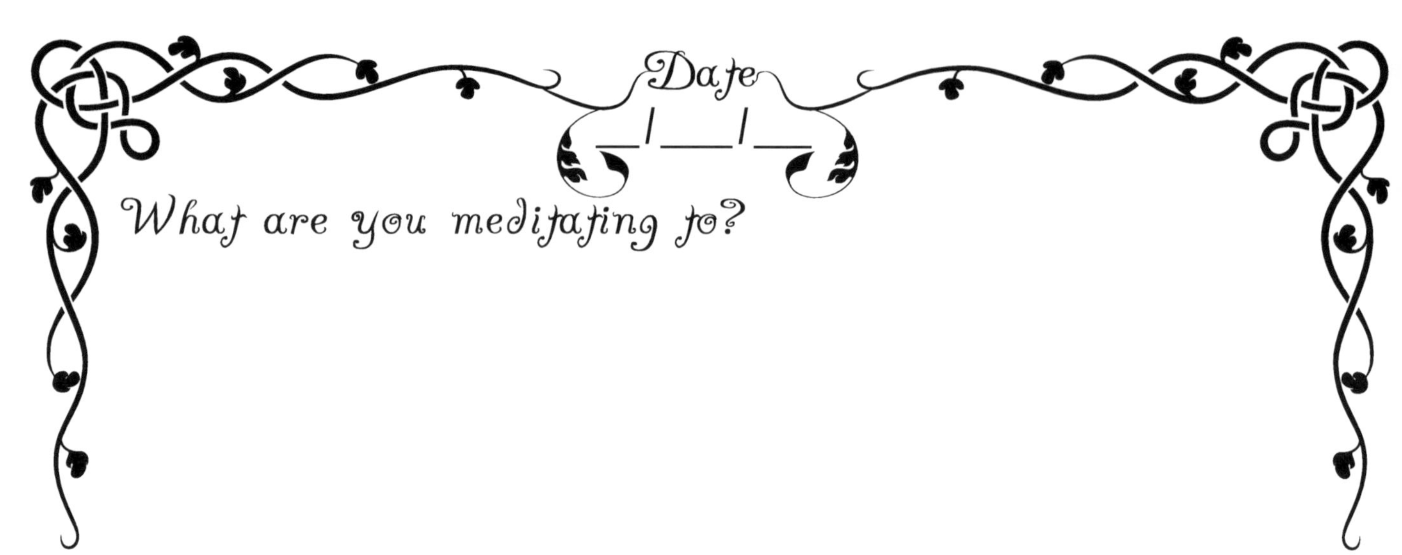

What are you meditating to?

How do you feel before meditation?

What did you smell?

What did you hear?

What did you see?

Reflection.

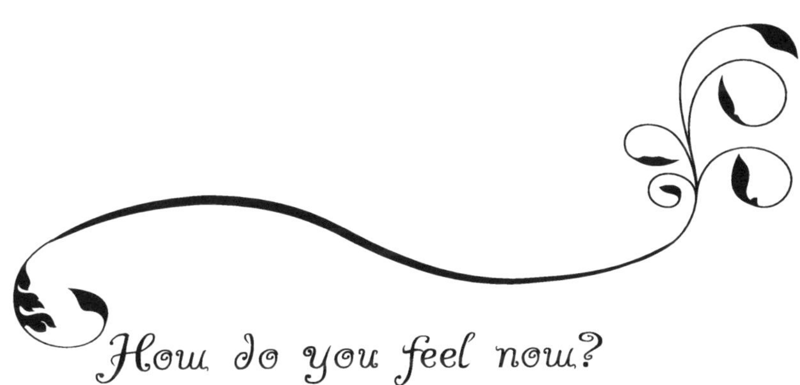

How do you feel now?

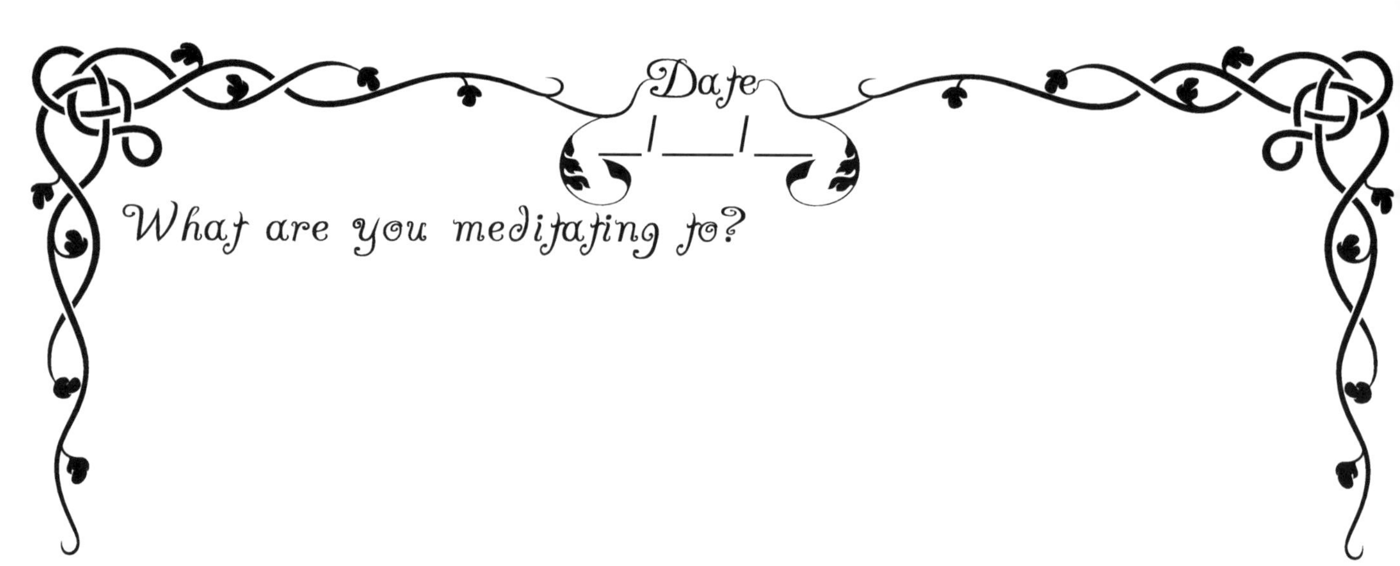

Date

__/__/__

What are you meditating to?

How do you feel before meditation?

What did you smell?

What did you hear?

What did you see?

Reflection.

How do you feel now?

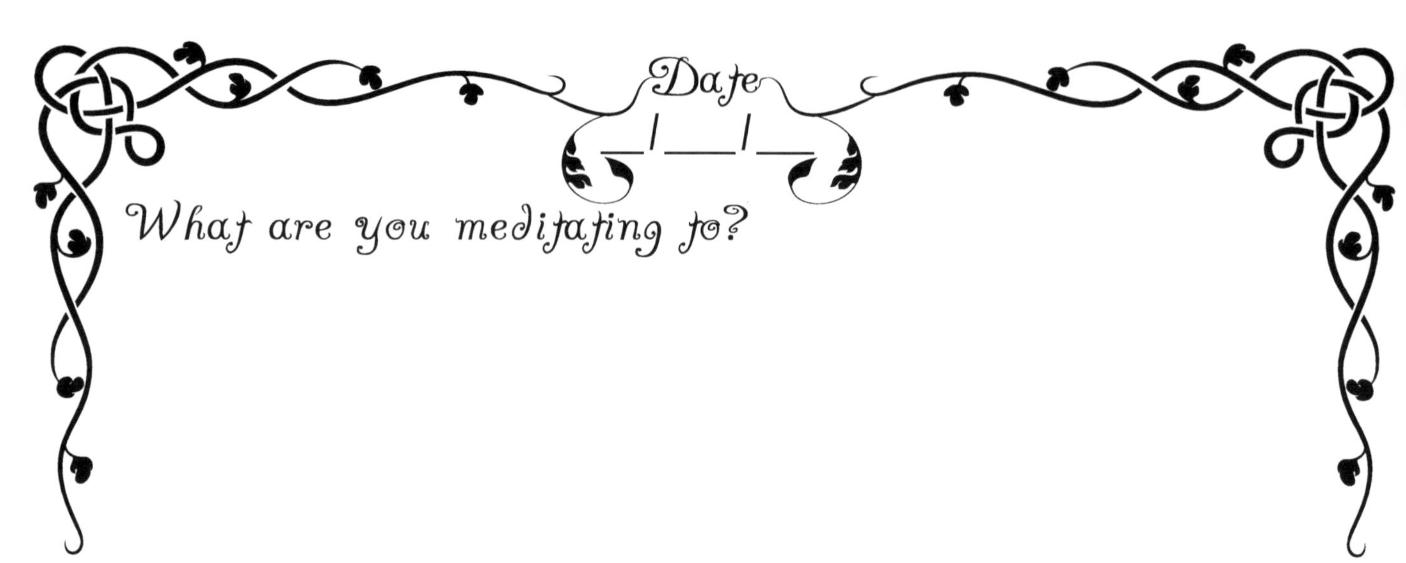

What are you meditating to?

How do you feel before meditation?

What did you smell?

What did you hear?

What did you see?

Reflection.

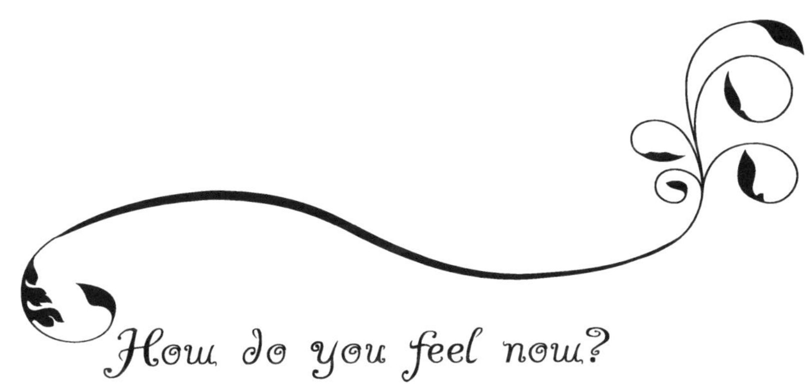

How do you feel now?

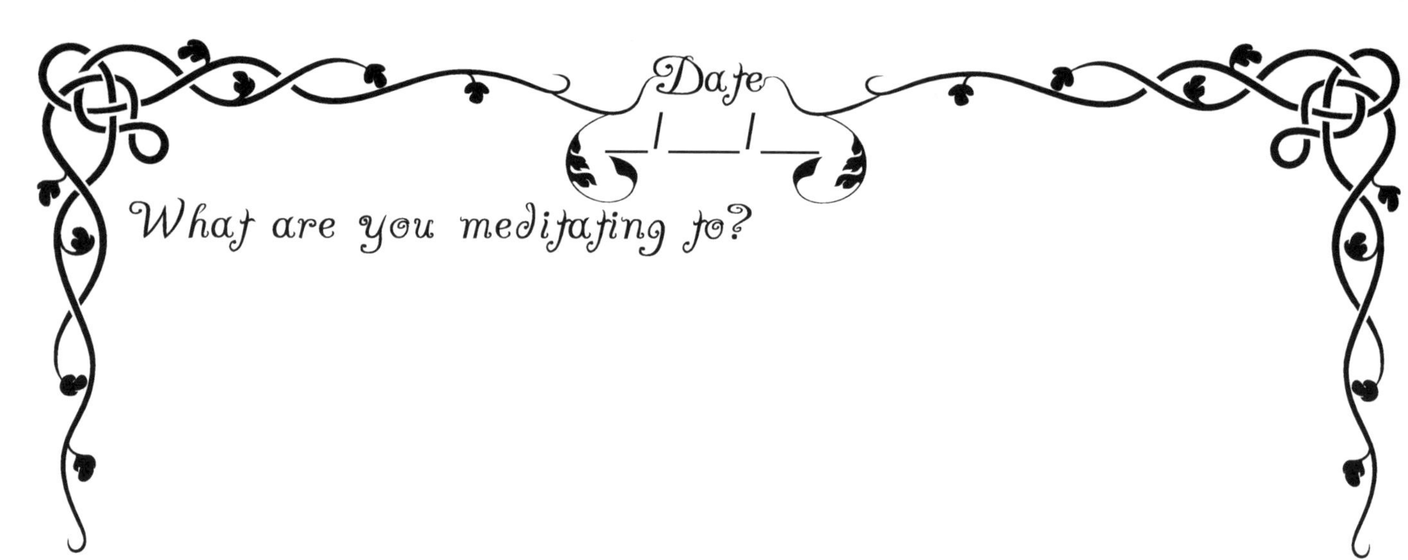

What are you meditating to?

How do you feel before meditation?

What did you smell?

What did you hear?

What did you see?

Reflection.

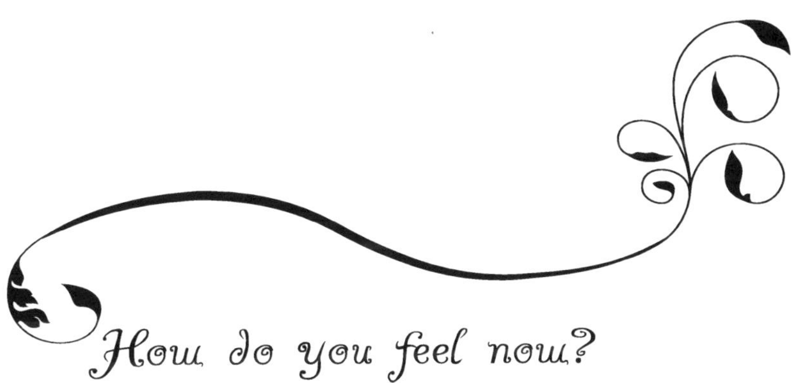

How do you feel now?

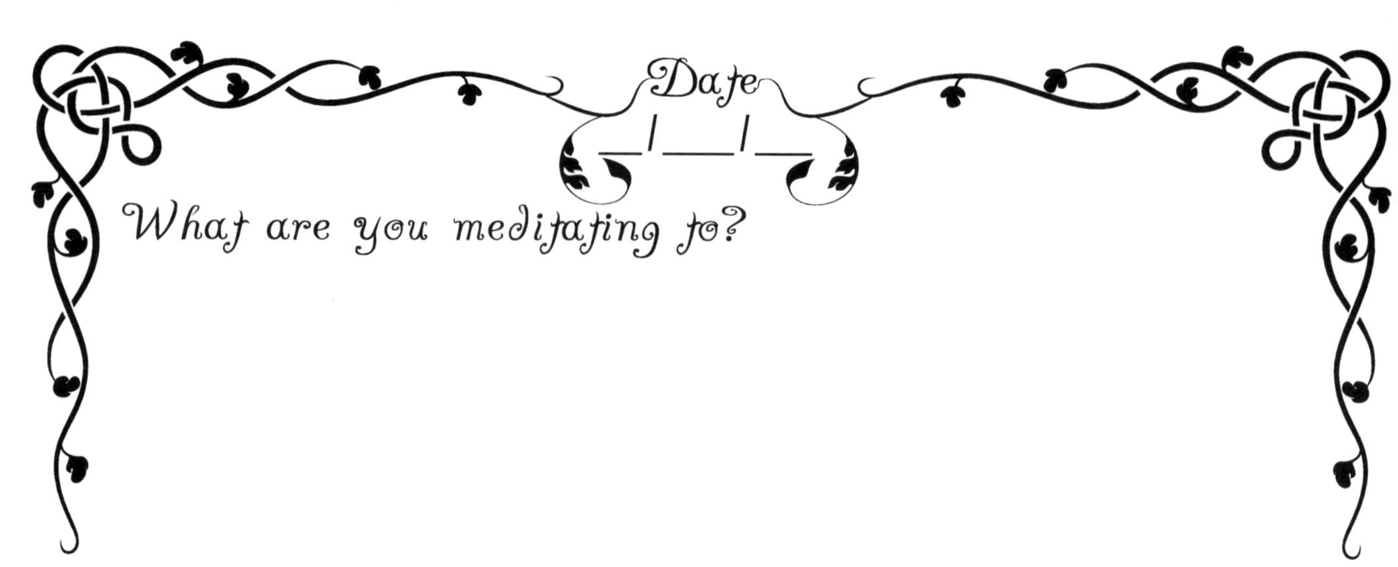

Date

__/__/__

What are you meditating to?

How do you feel before meditation?

What did you smell?

What did you hear?

What did you see?

Reflection.

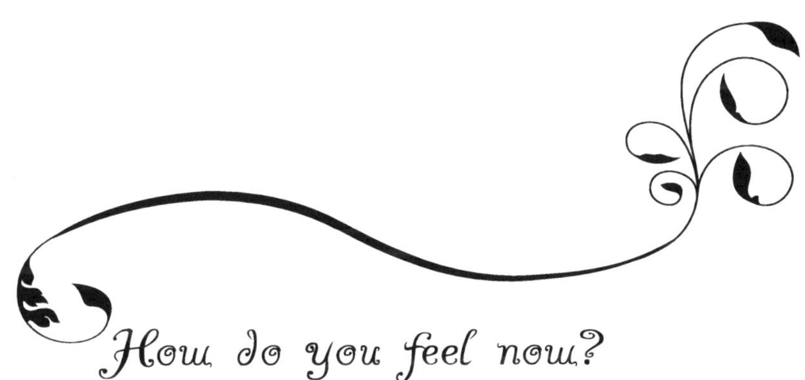

How do you feel now?

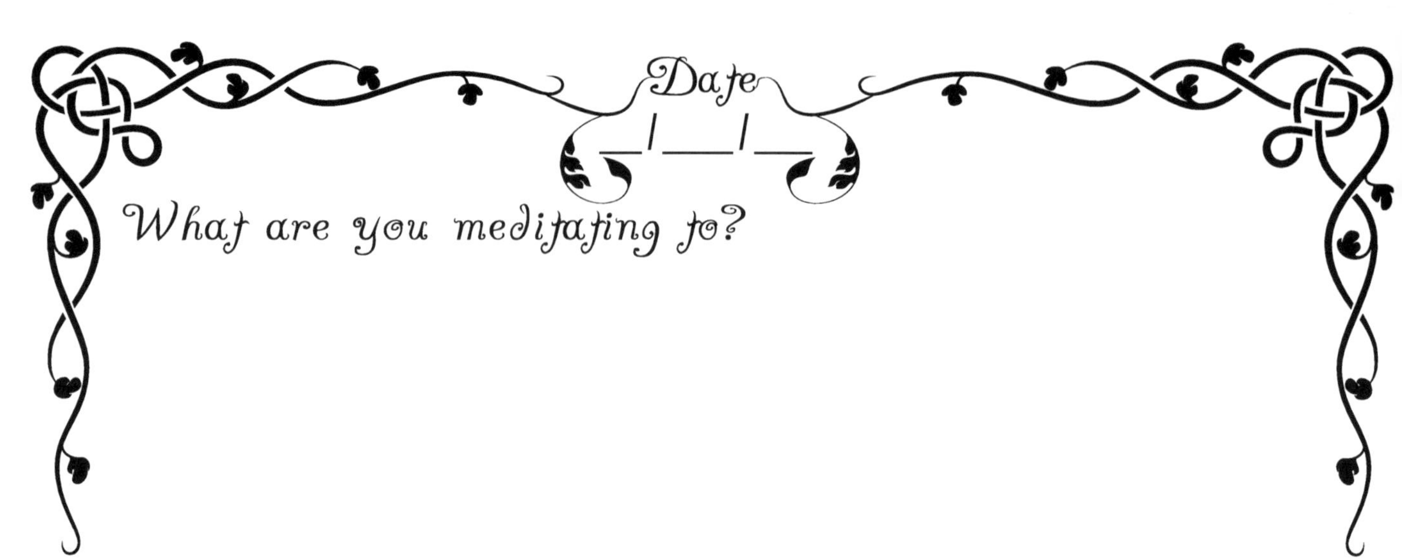

Date

__/___/__

What are you meditating to?

How do you feel before meditation?

What did you smell?

What did you hear?

What did you see?

Reflection.

How do you feel now?

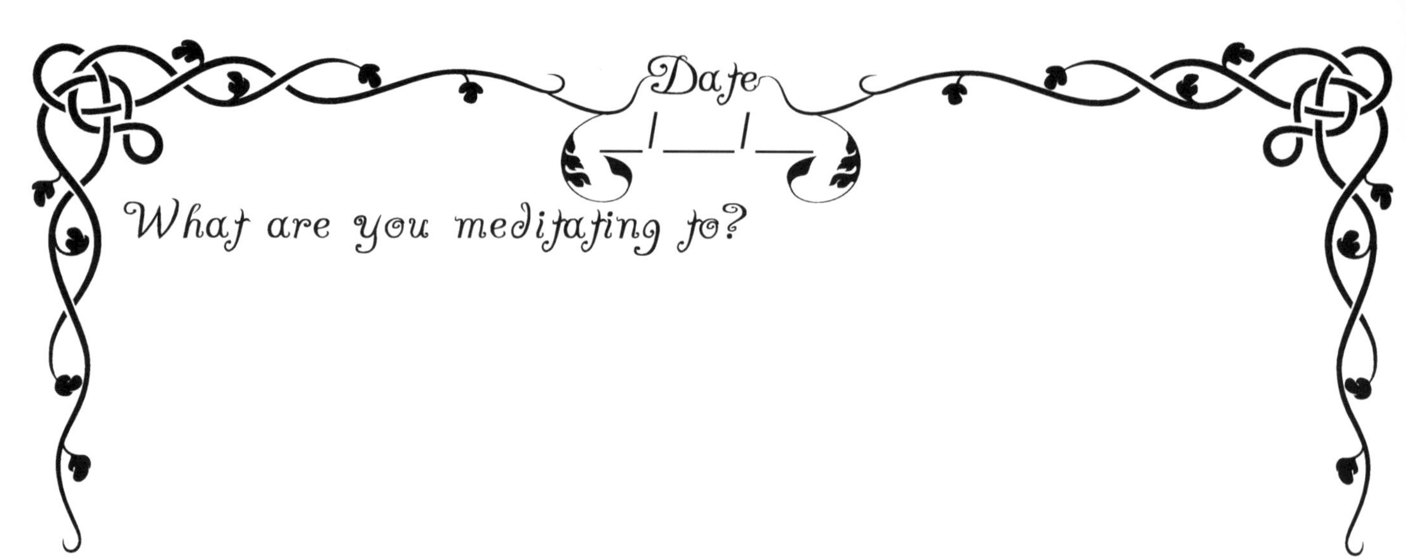

Date
__/__/__

What are you meditating to?

How do you feel before meditation?

What did you smell?

What did you hear?

What did you see?

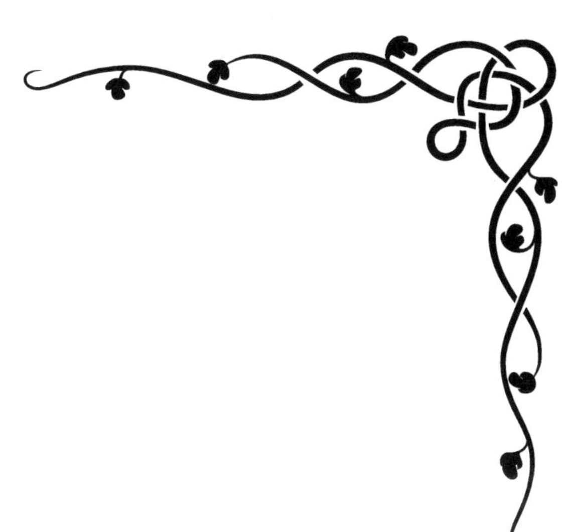

Reflection.

How do you feel now?

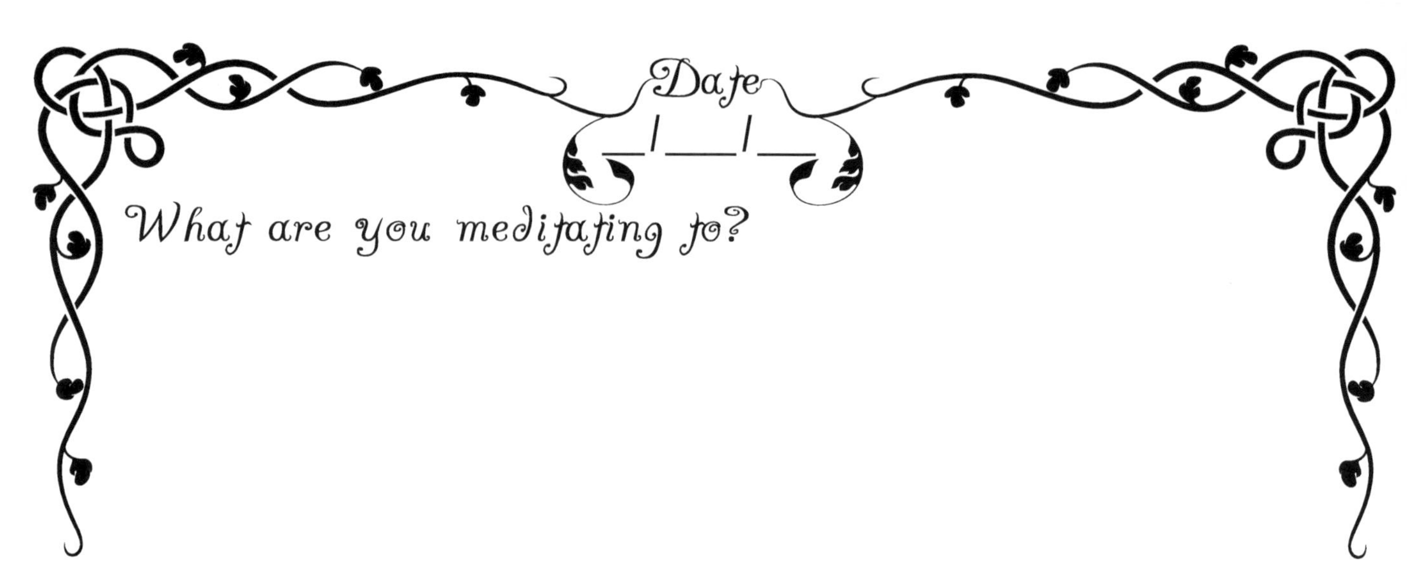

Date

__/__/__

What are you meditating to?

How do you feel before meditation?

What did you smell?

What did you hear?

What did you see?

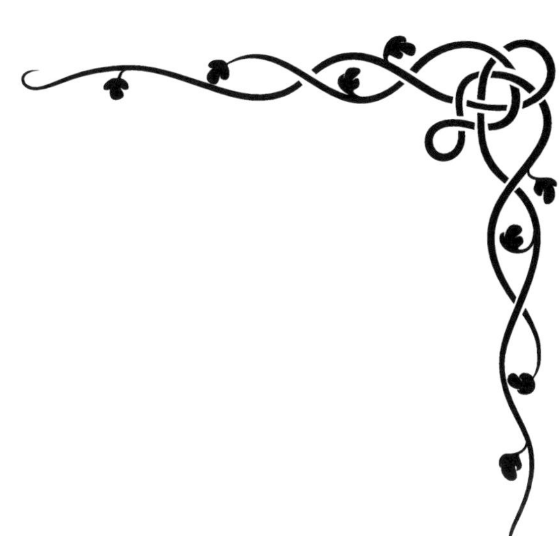

Reflection.

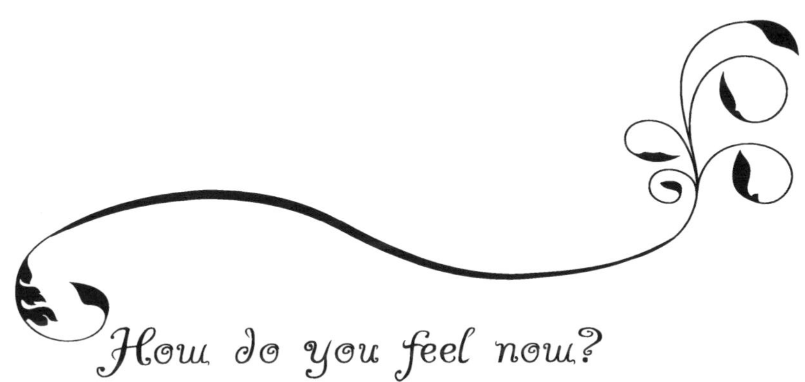

How do you feel now?

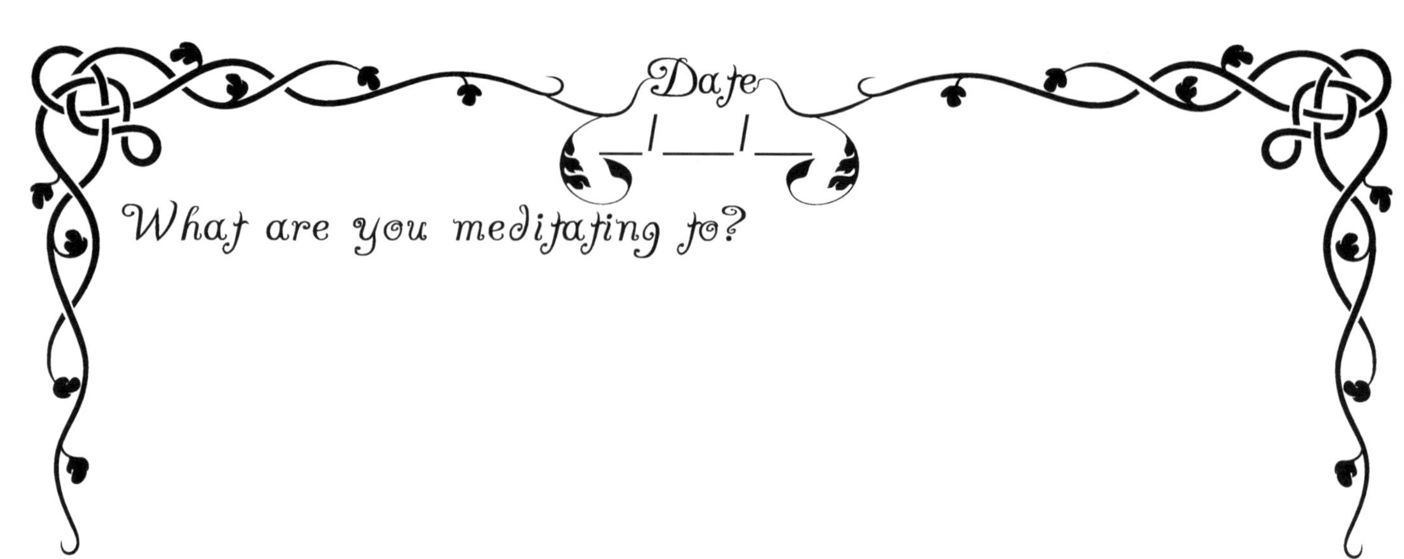

Date

__/__/__

What are you meditating to?

How do you feel before meditation?

What did you smell?

What did you hear?

What did you see?

Reflection.

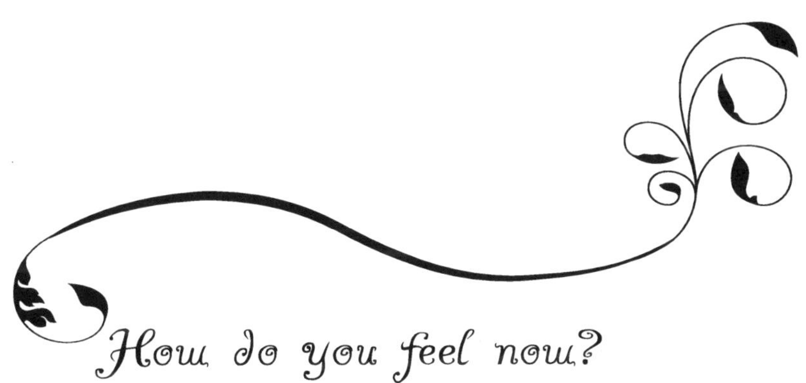

How do you feel now?

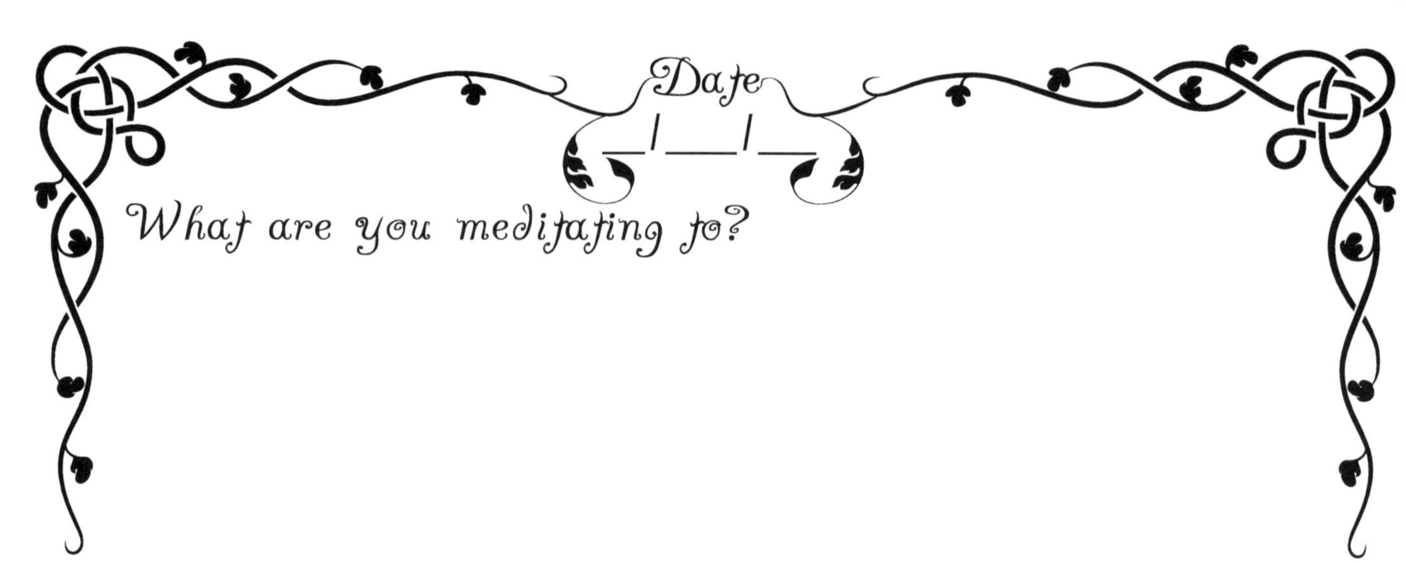

Date

__/___/__

What are you meditating to?

How do you feel before meditation?

What did you smell?

What did you hear?

What did you see?

Reflection.

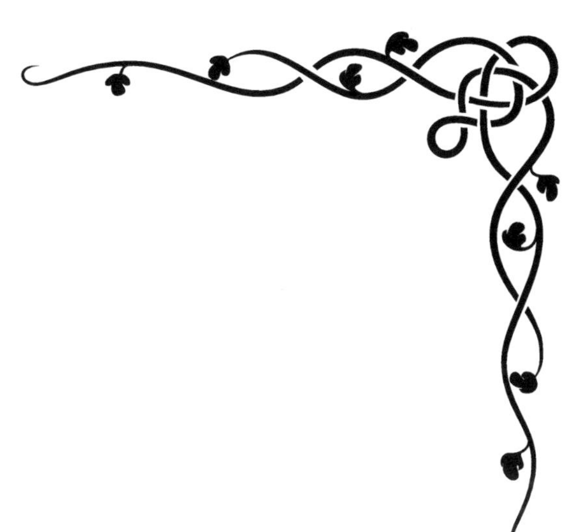

How do you feel now?

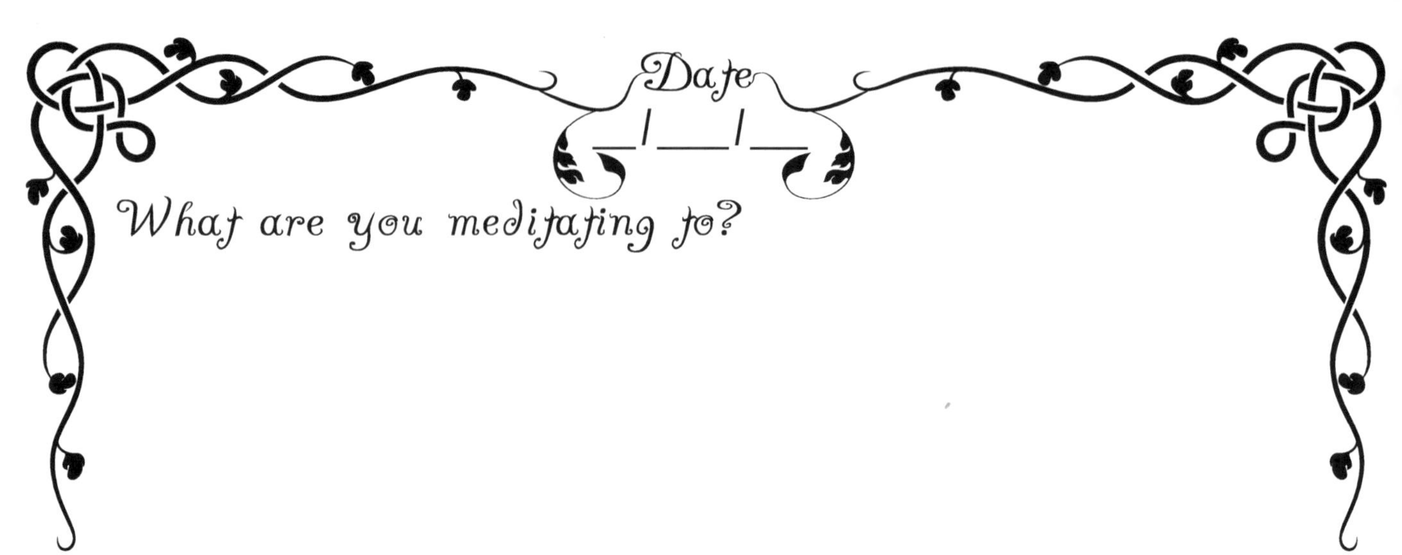

What are you meditating to?

How do you feel before meditation?

What did you smell?

What did you hear?

What did you see?

Reflection.

How do you feel now?

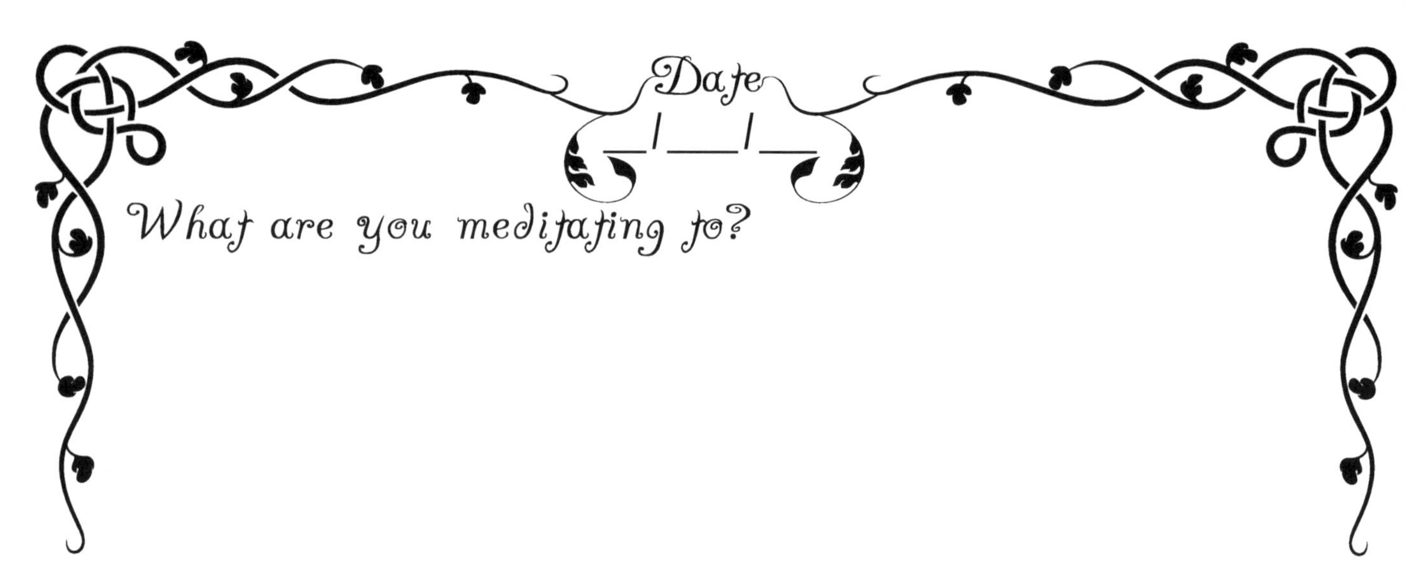

Date

__/__/__

What are you meditating to?

How do you feel before meditation?

What did you smell?

What did you hear?

What did you see?

Reflection.

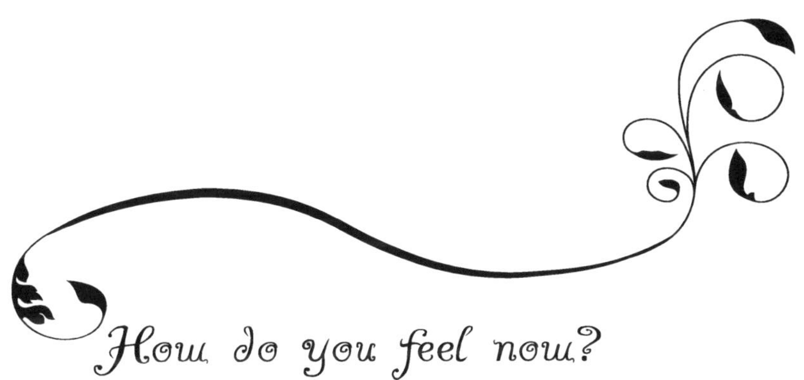

How do you feel now?

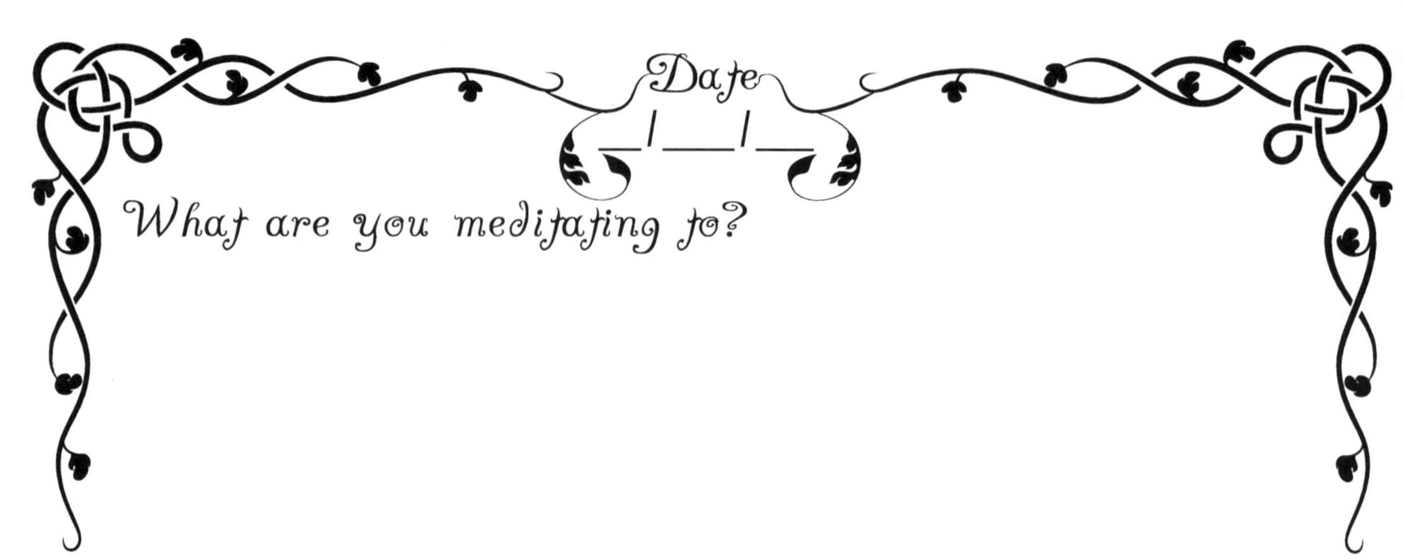

Date
__/__/__

What are you meditating to?

How do you feel before meditation?

What did you smell?

What did you hear?

What did you see?

Reflection.

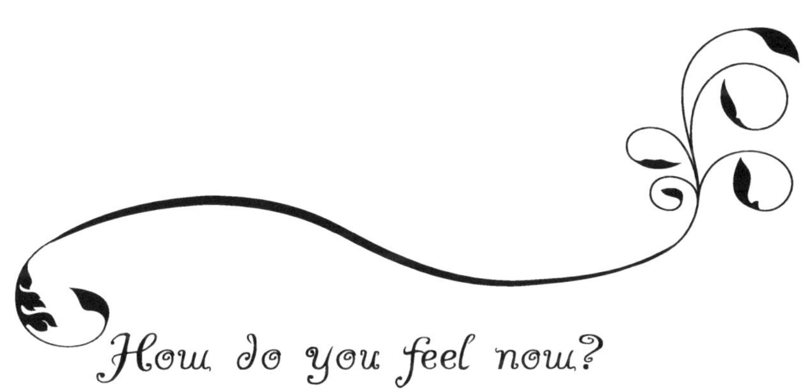

How do you feel now?

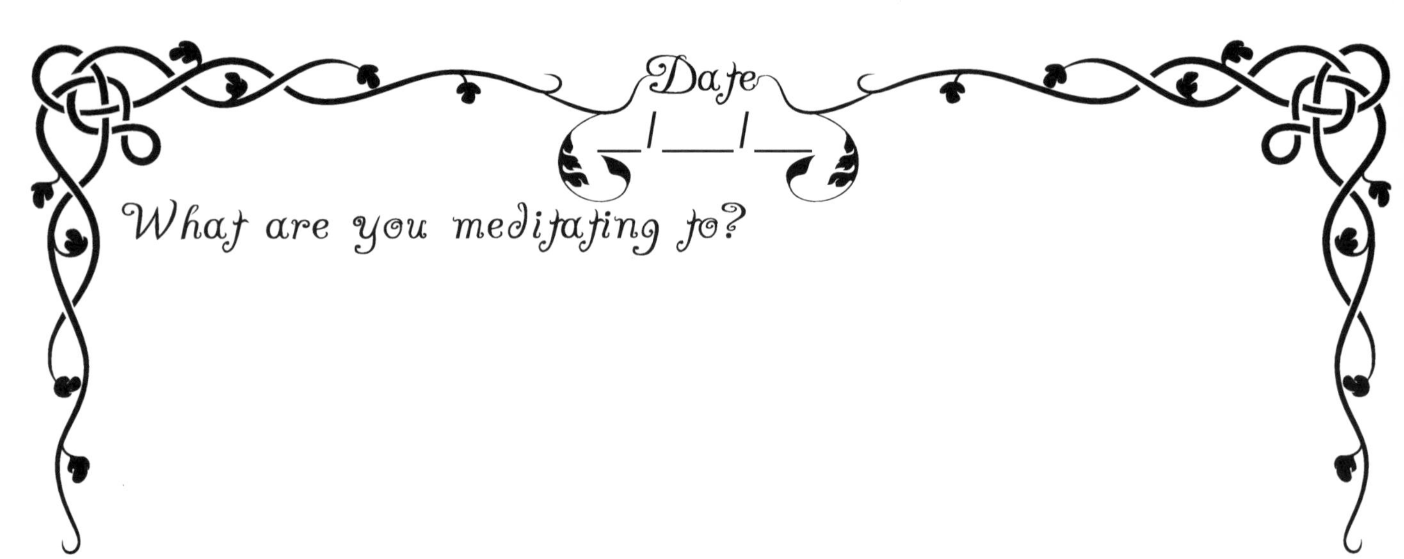

Date
__/____/____

What are you meditating to?

How do you feel before meditation?

What did you smell?

What did you hear?

What did you see?

Reflection.

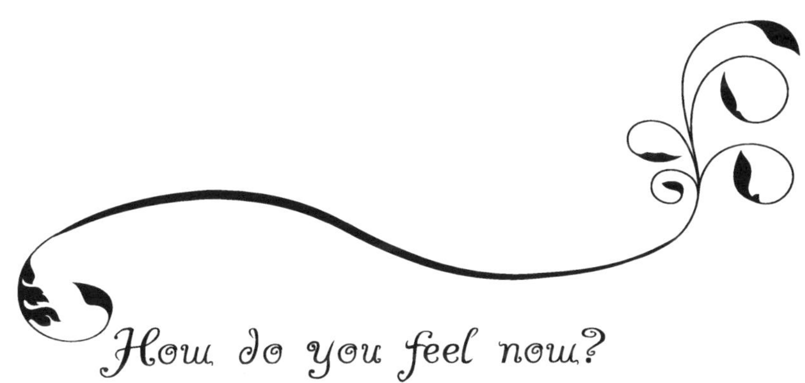

How do you feel now?

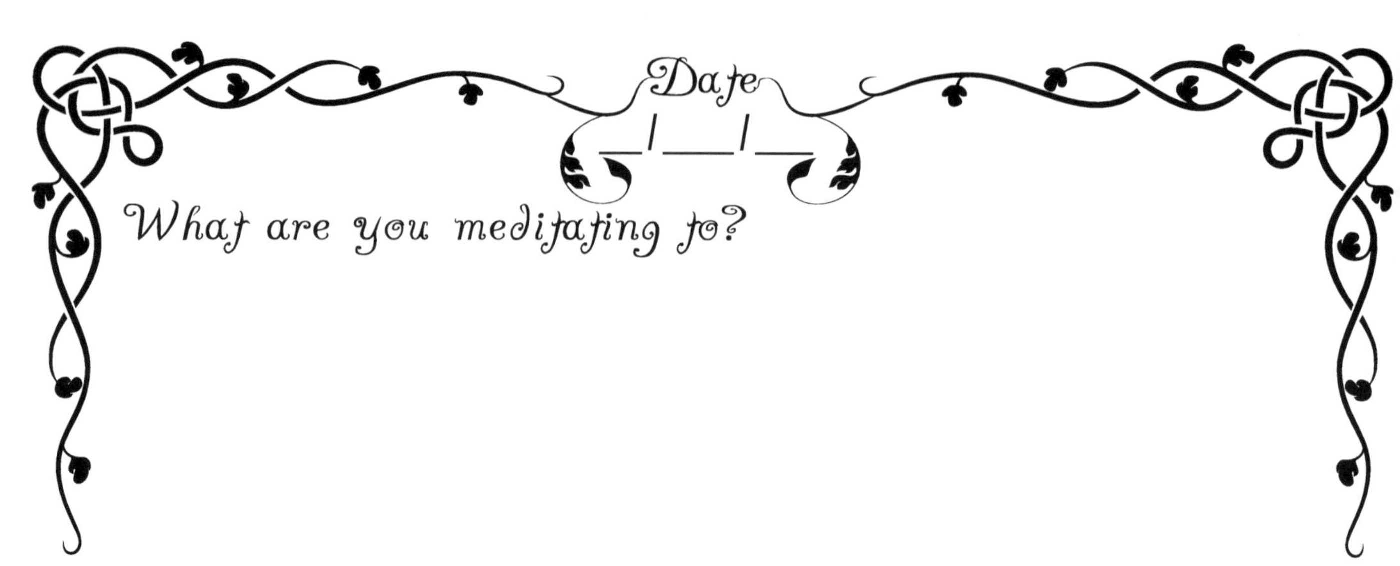

Date __/__/__

What are you meditating to?

How do you feel before meditation?

What did you smell?

What did you hear?

What did you see?

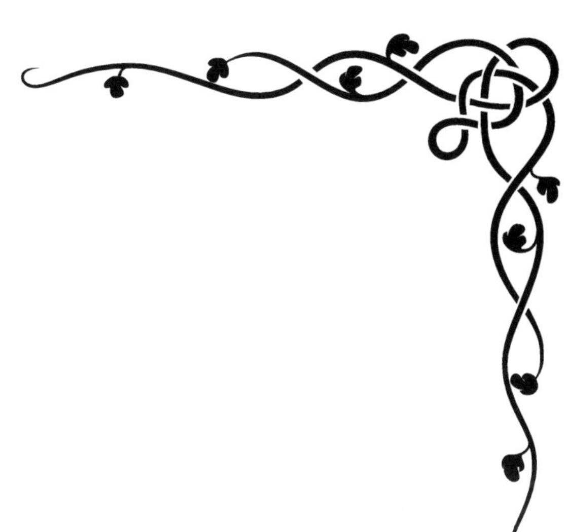

Reflection.

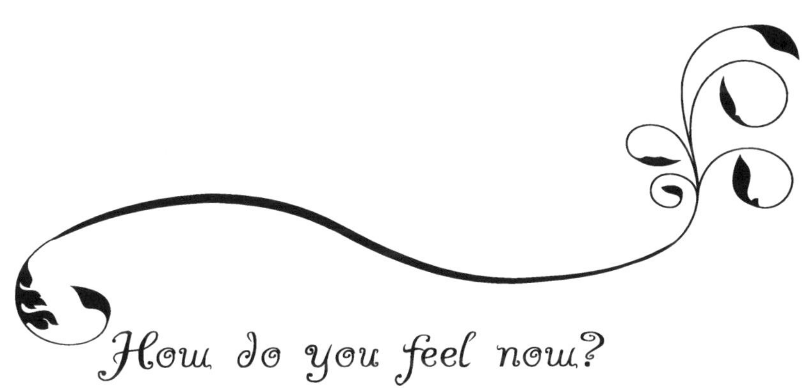

How do you feel now?

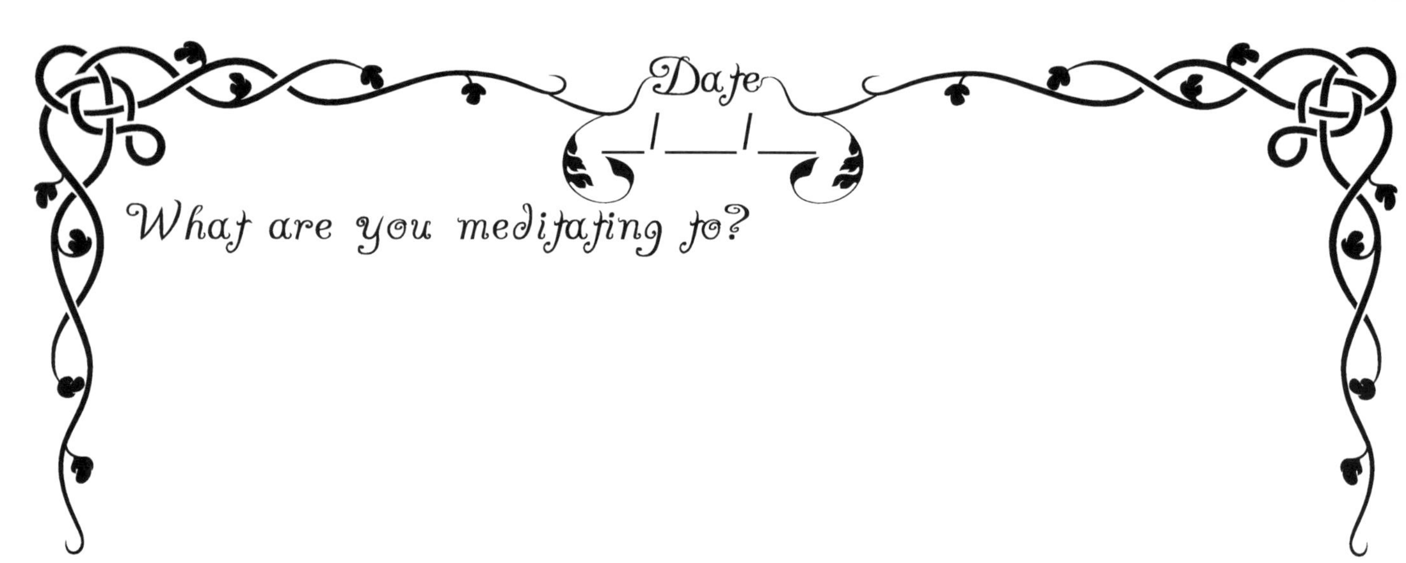

What are you meditating to?

How do you feel before meditation?

What did you smell?

What did you hear?

What did you see?

Reflection.

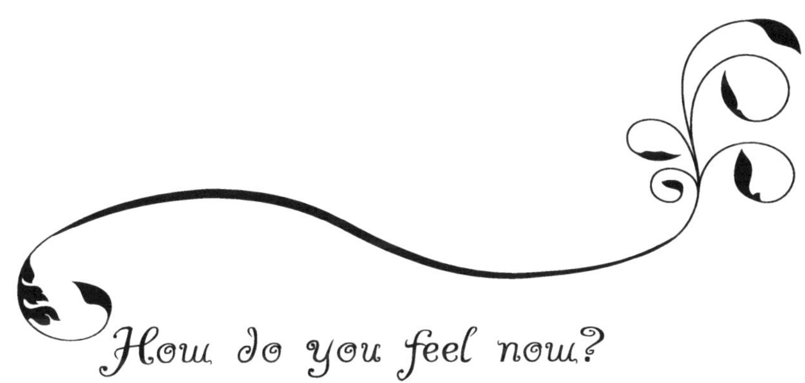

How do you feel now?

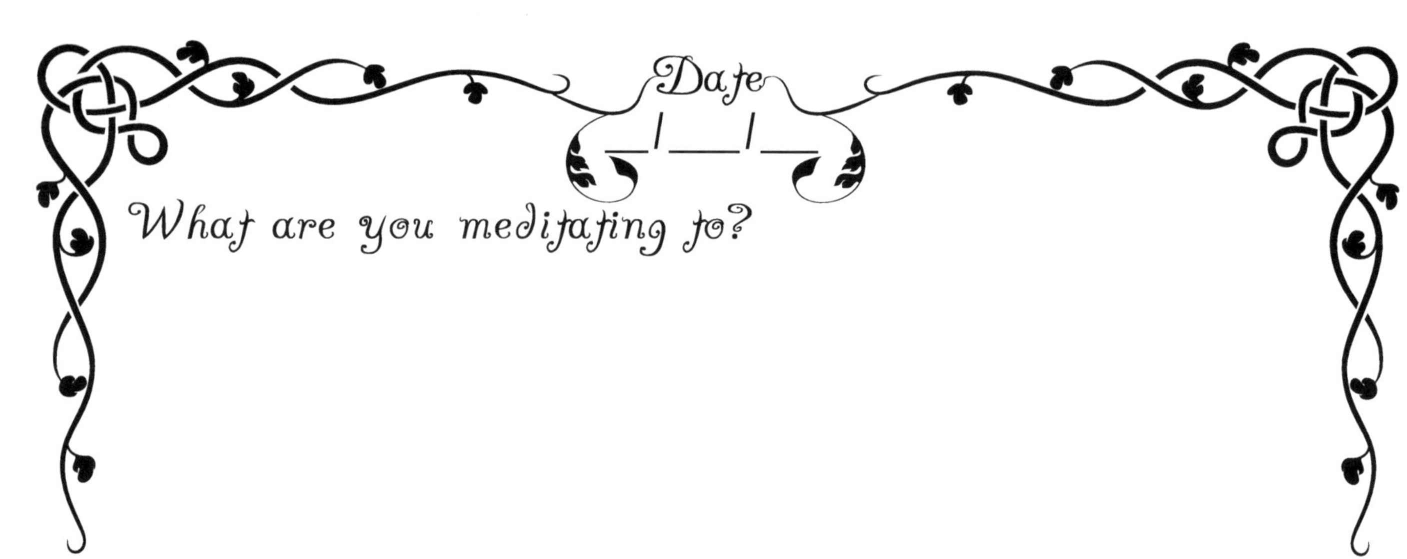

Date

__/__/__

What are you meditating to?

How do you feel before meditation?

What did you smell?

What did you hear?

What did you see?

Reflection.

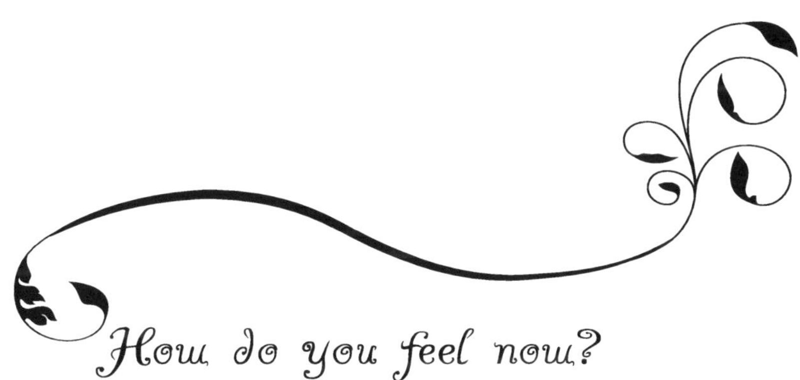

How do you feel now?

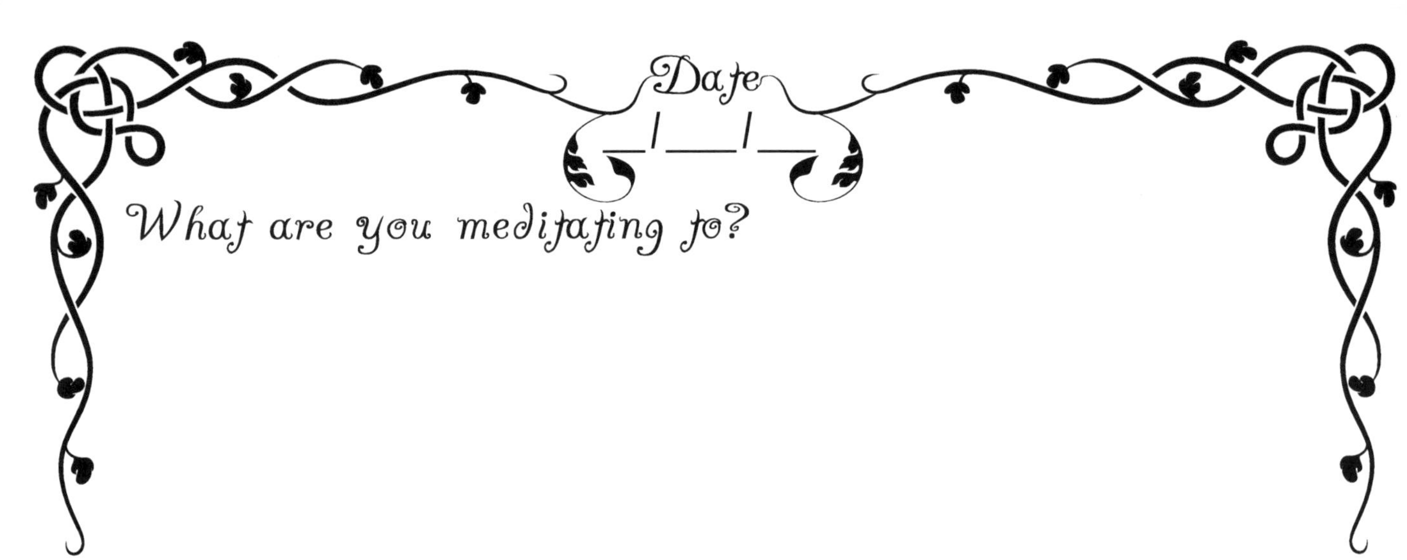

Date
__/__/__

What are you meditating to?

How do you feel before meditation?

What did you smell?

What did you hear?

What did you see?

Reflection.

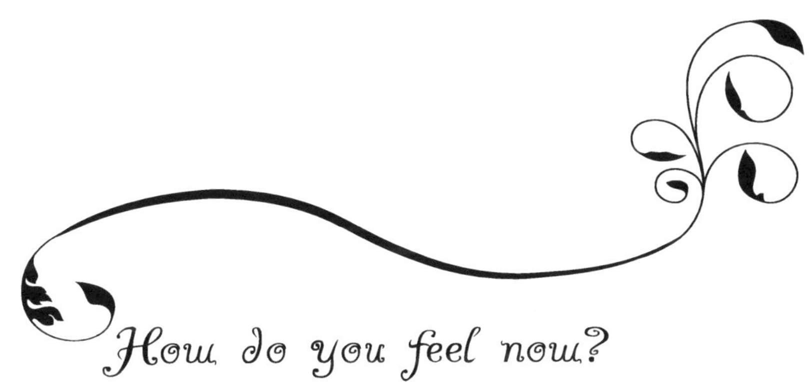

How do you feel now?

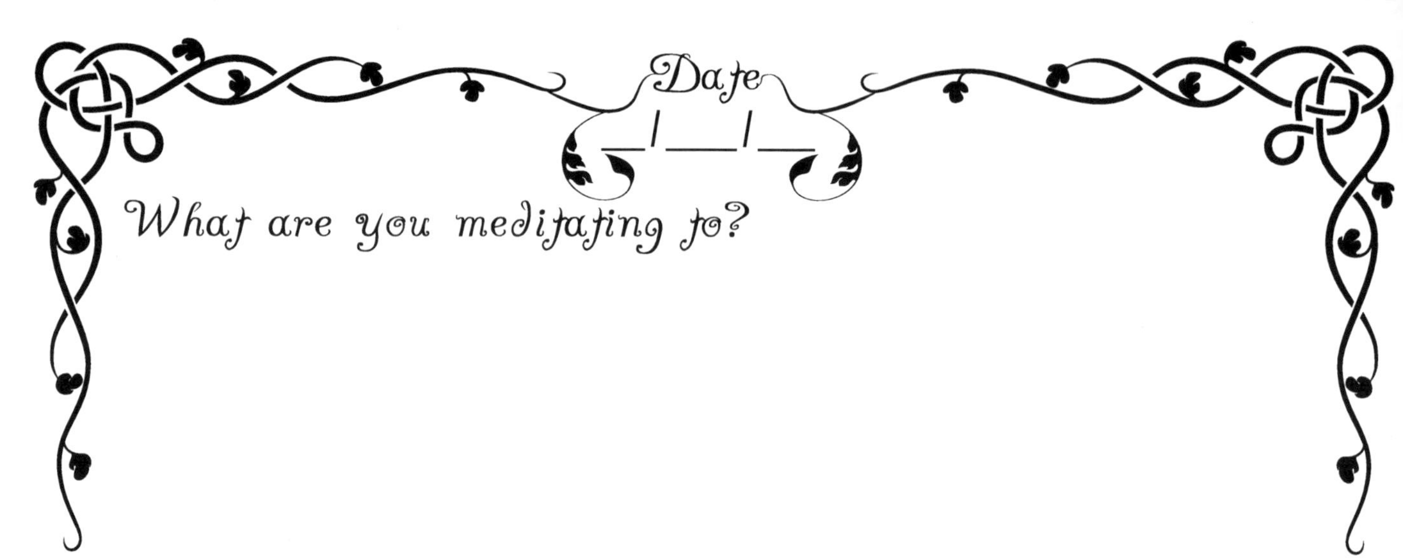

Date
__/____/___

What are you meditating to?

How do you feel before meditation?

What did you smell?

What did you hear?

What did you see?

Reflection.

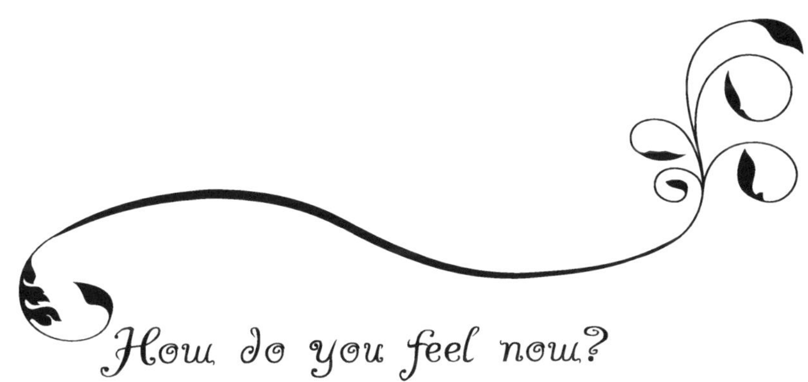

How do you feel now?

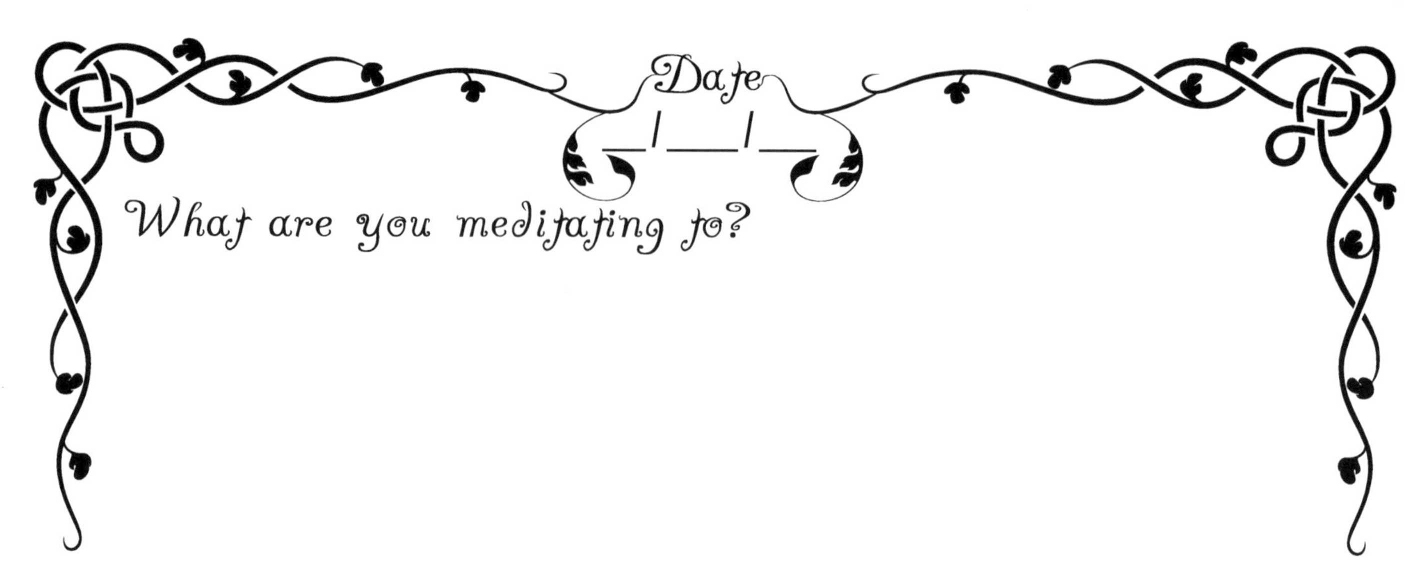

Date

__/__/__

What are you meditating to?

How do you feel before meditation?

What did you smell?

What did you hear?

What did you see?

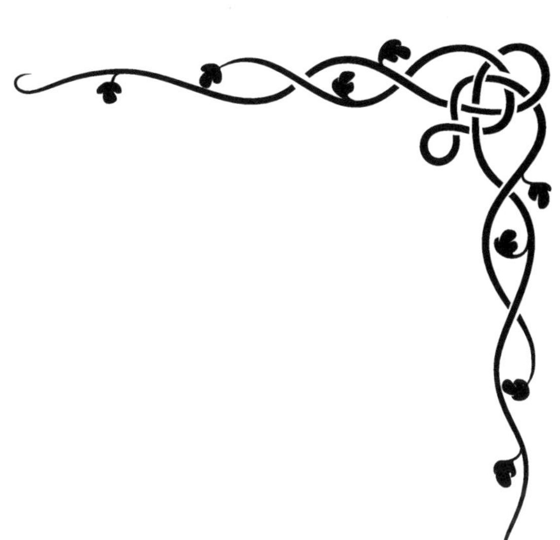

Reflection.

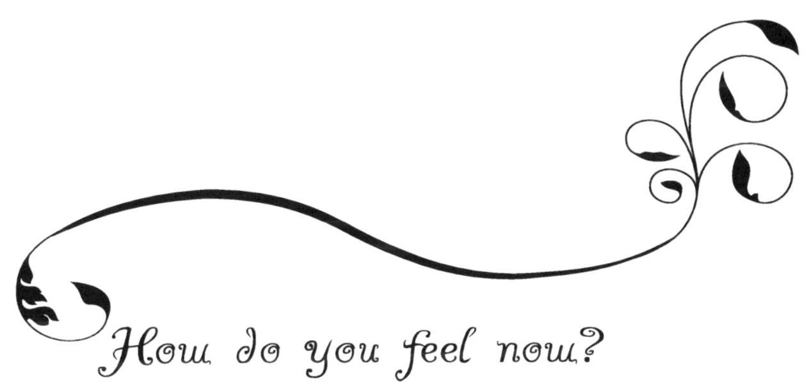

How do you feel now?

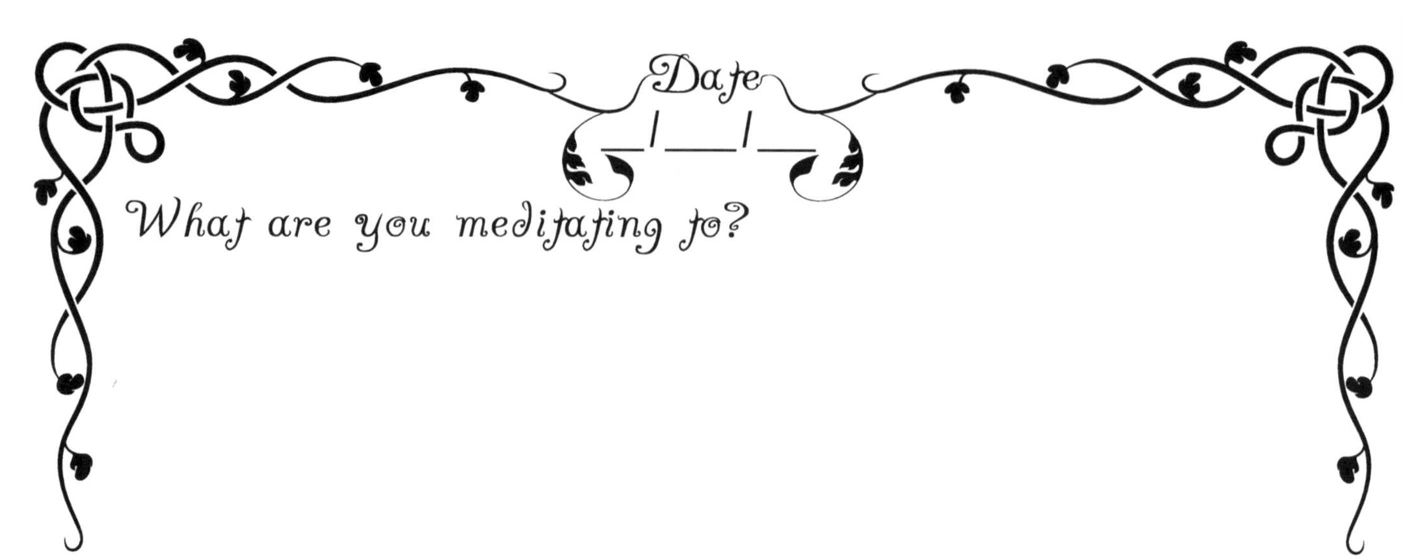

Date

__/__/__

What are you meditating to?

How do you feel before meditation?

What did you smell?

What did you hear?

What did you see?

Reflection.

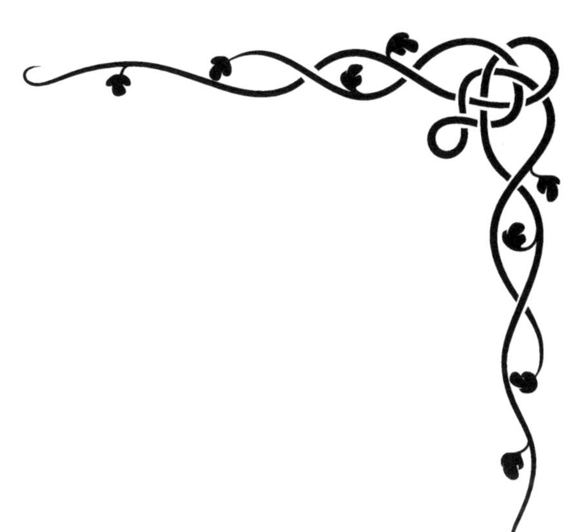

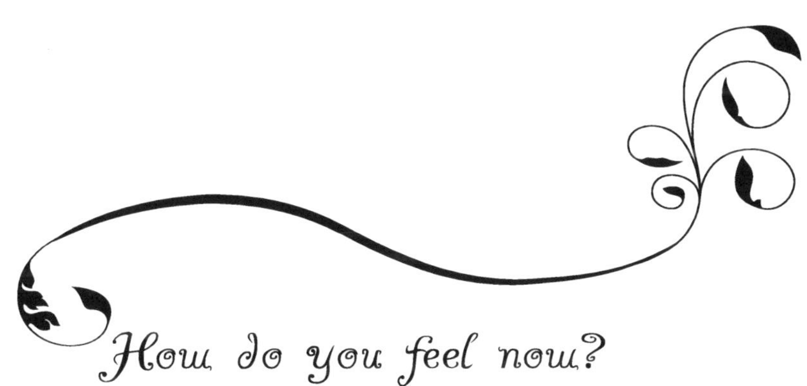

How do you feel now?

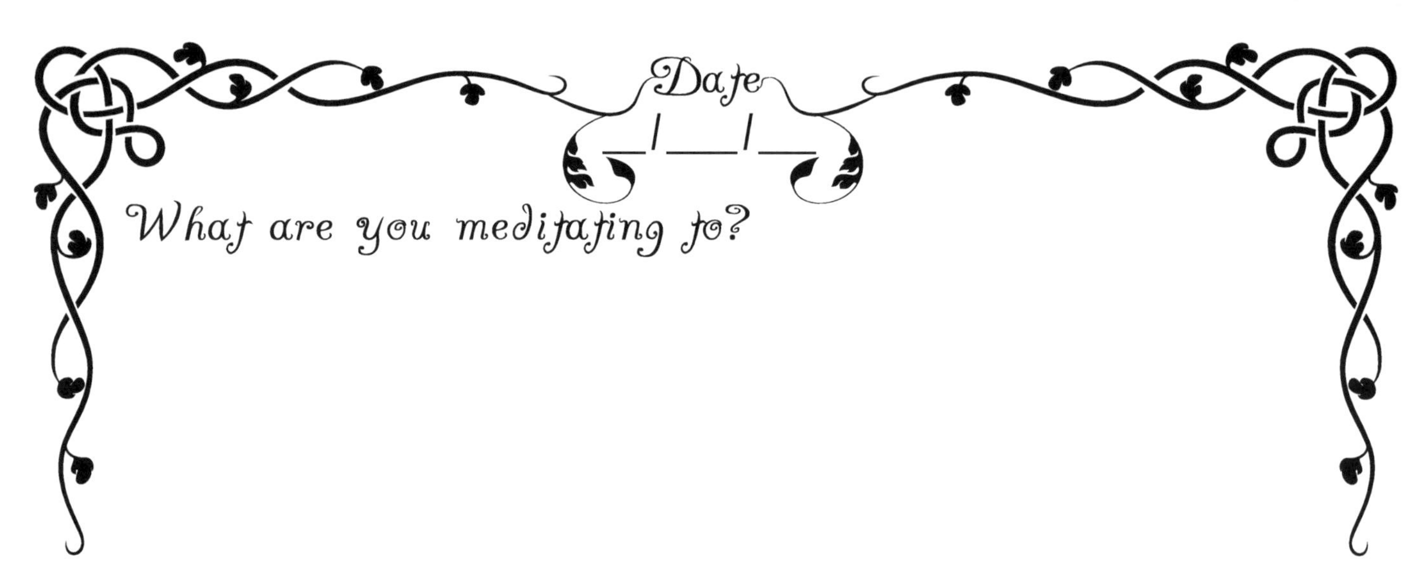

Date

___/___/___

What are you meditating to?

How do you feel before meditation?

What did you smell?

What did you hear?

What did you see?

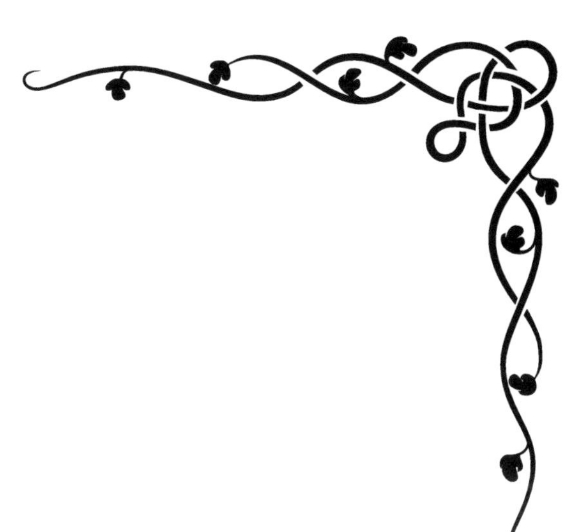

Reflection.

How do you feel now?

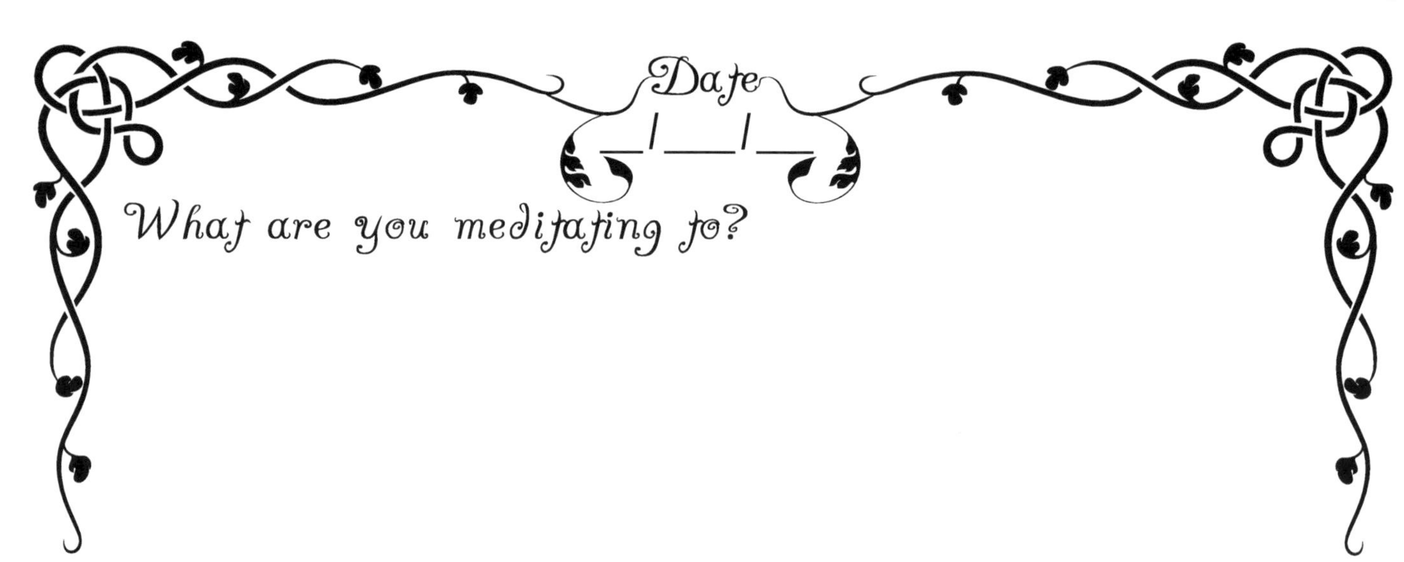

Date
__/__/__

What are you meditating to?

How do you feel before meditation?

What did you smell?

What did you hear?

What did you see?

Reflection.

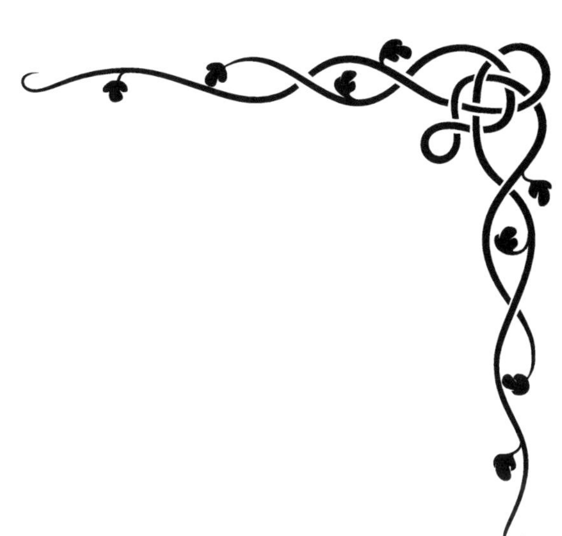

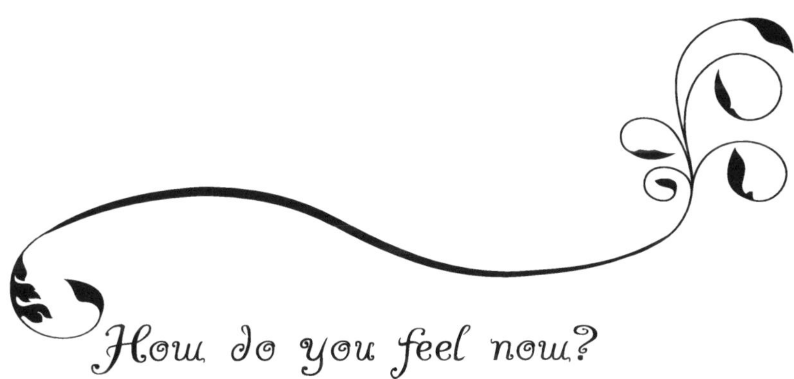

How do you feel now?

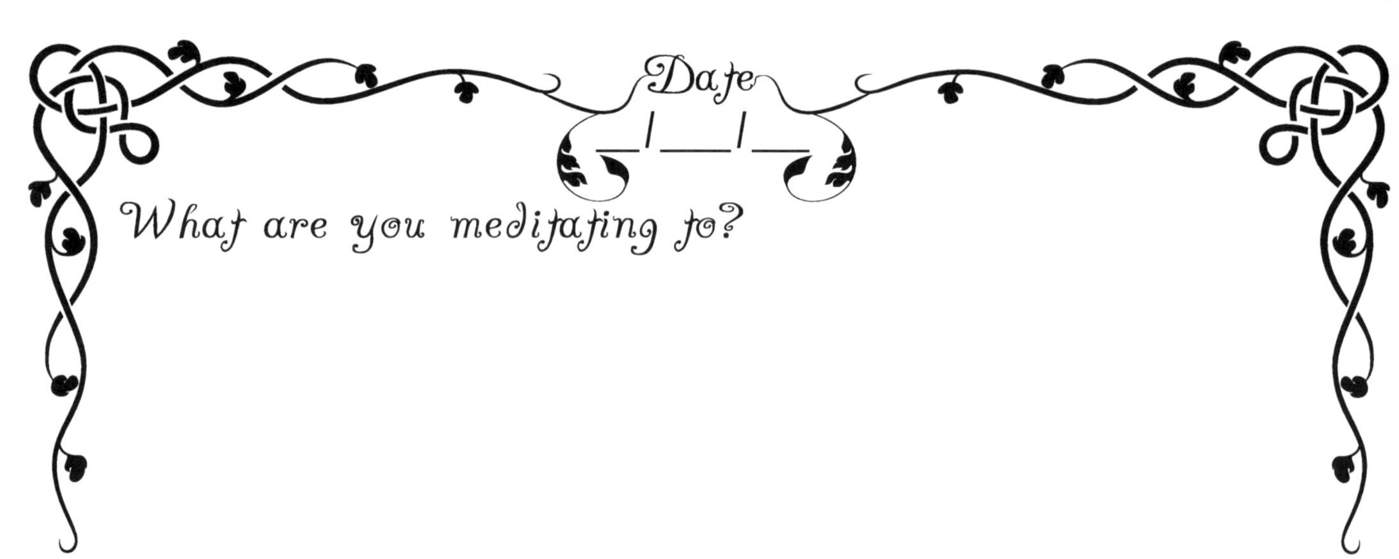

What are you meditating to?

How do you feel before meditation?

What did you smell?

What did you hear?

What did you see?

Reflection.

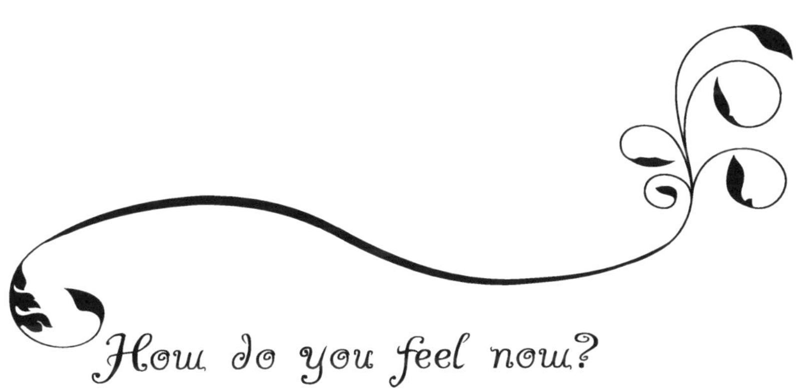

How do you feel now?

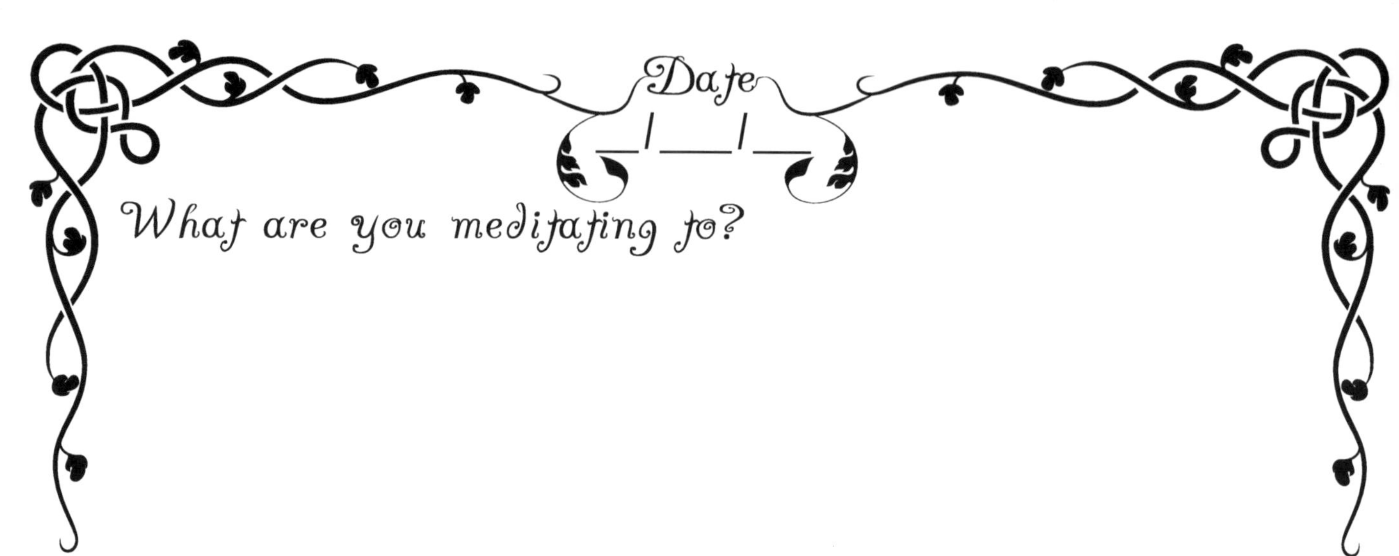

Date

__/___/___

What are you meditating to?

How do you feel before meditation?

What did you smell?

What did you hear?

What did you see?

Reflection.

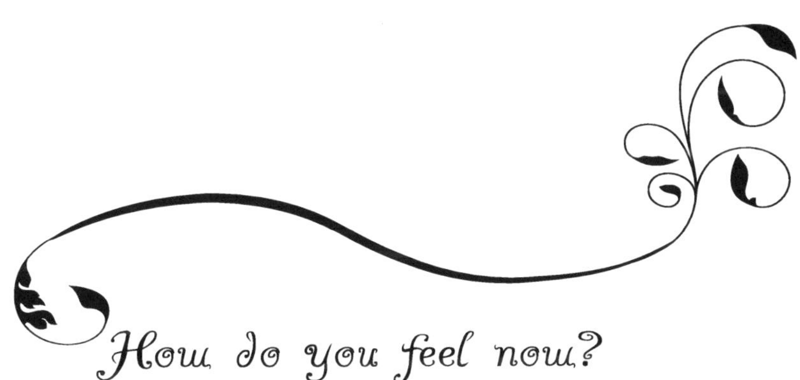

How do you feel now?

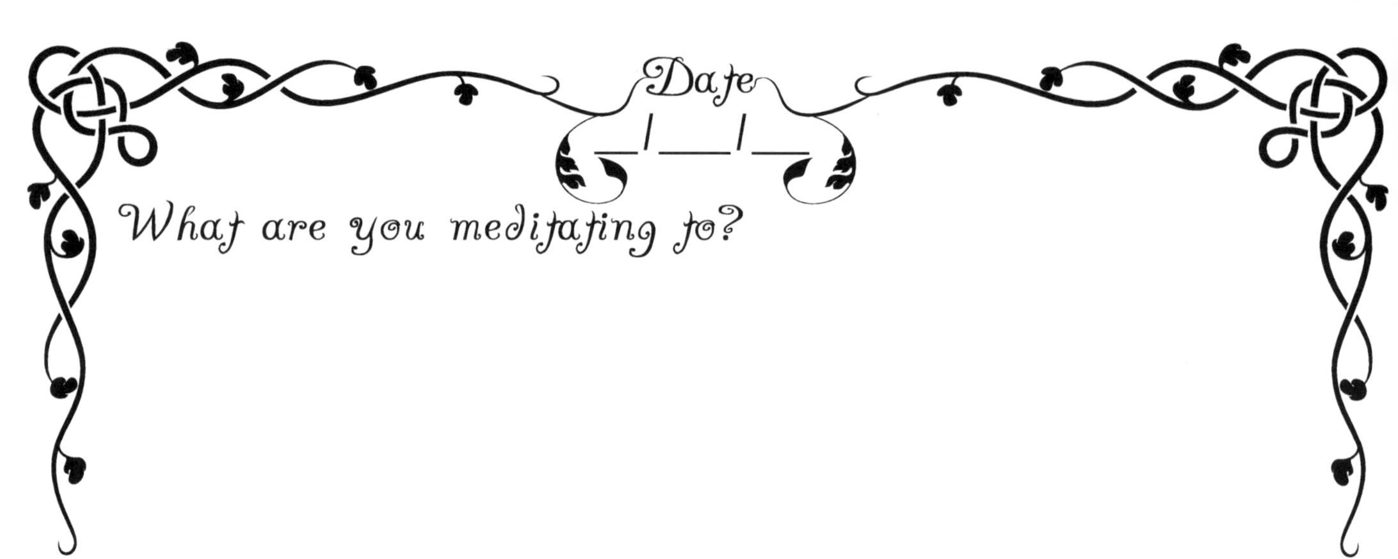

Date
__/__/__

What are you meditating to?

How do you feel before meditation?

What did you smell?

What did you hear?

What did you see?

Reflection.

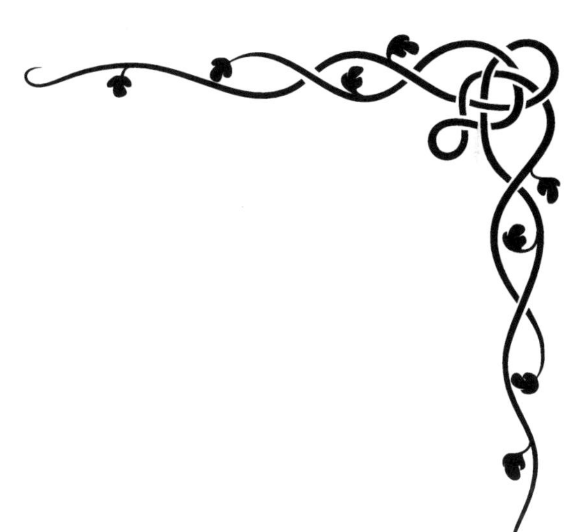

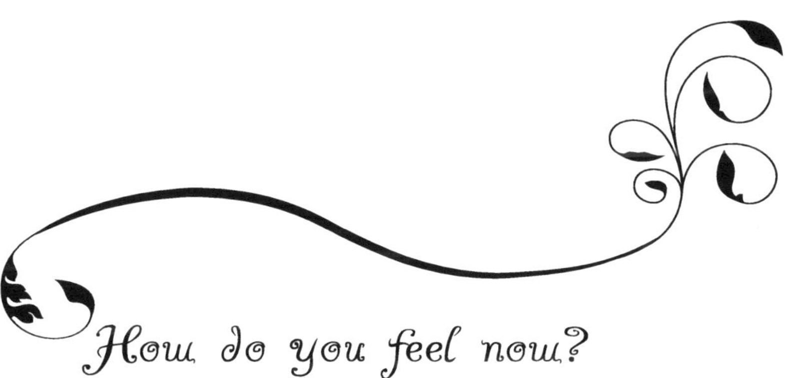

How do you feel now?

What are you meditating to?

How do you feel before meditation?

What did you smell?

What did you hear?

What did you see?

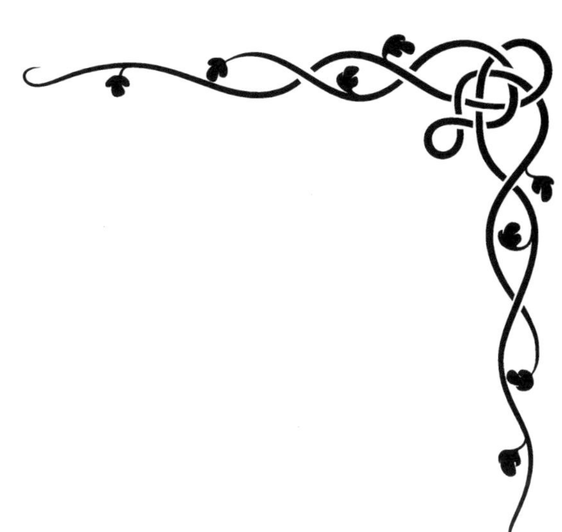

Reflection.

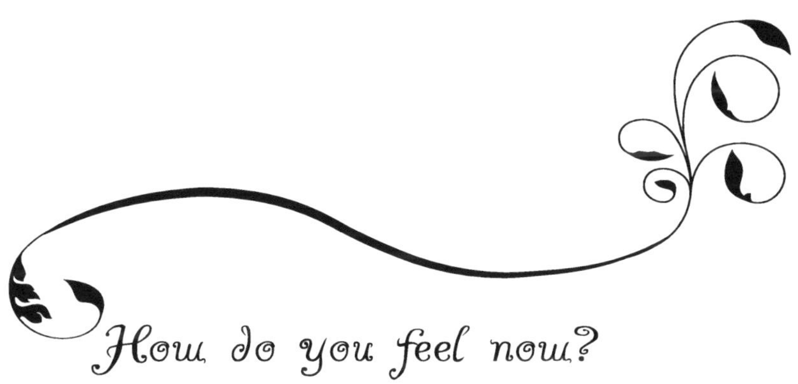

How do you feel now?

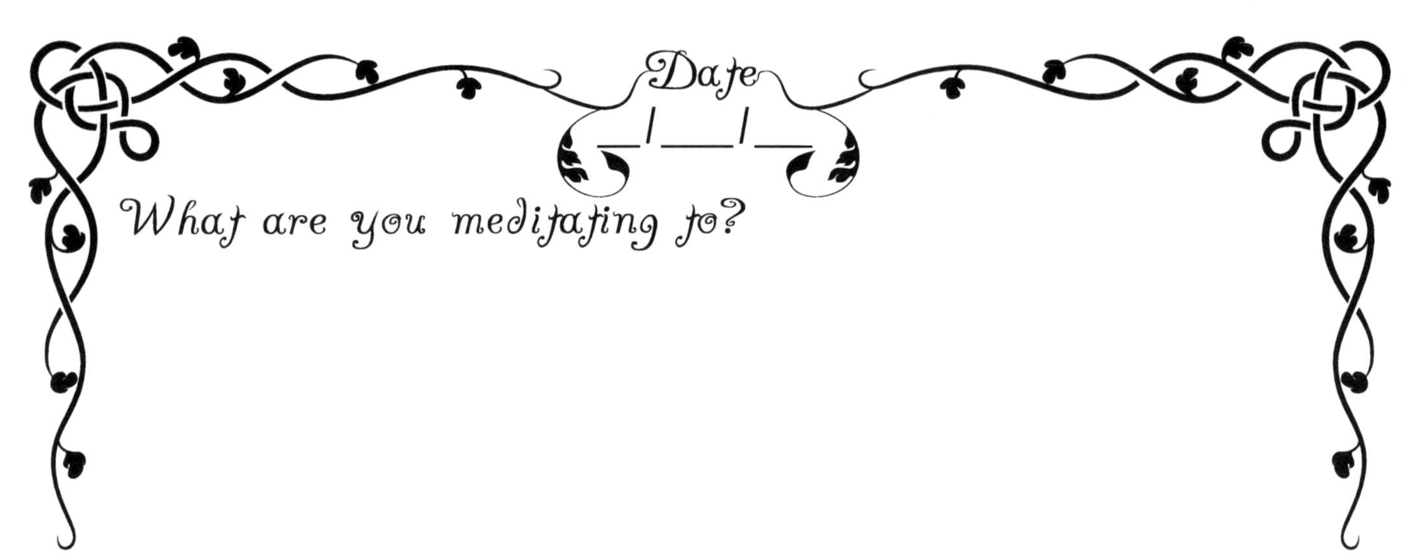

Date

__/__/__

What are you meditating to?

How do you feel before meditation?

What did you smell?

What did you hear?

What did you see?

Reflection.

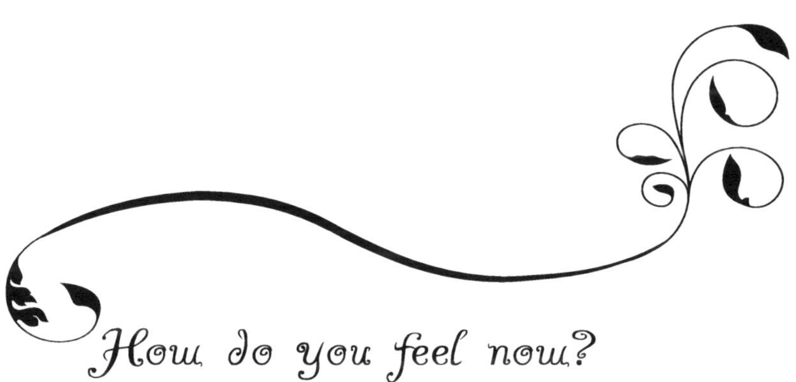

How do you feel now?

Date
__/__/__

What are you meditating to?

How do you feel before meditation?

What did you smell?

What did you hear?

What did you see?

Reflection.

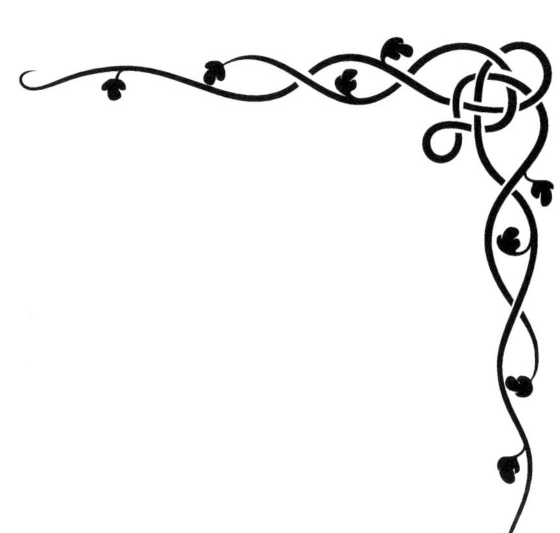

How do you feel now?

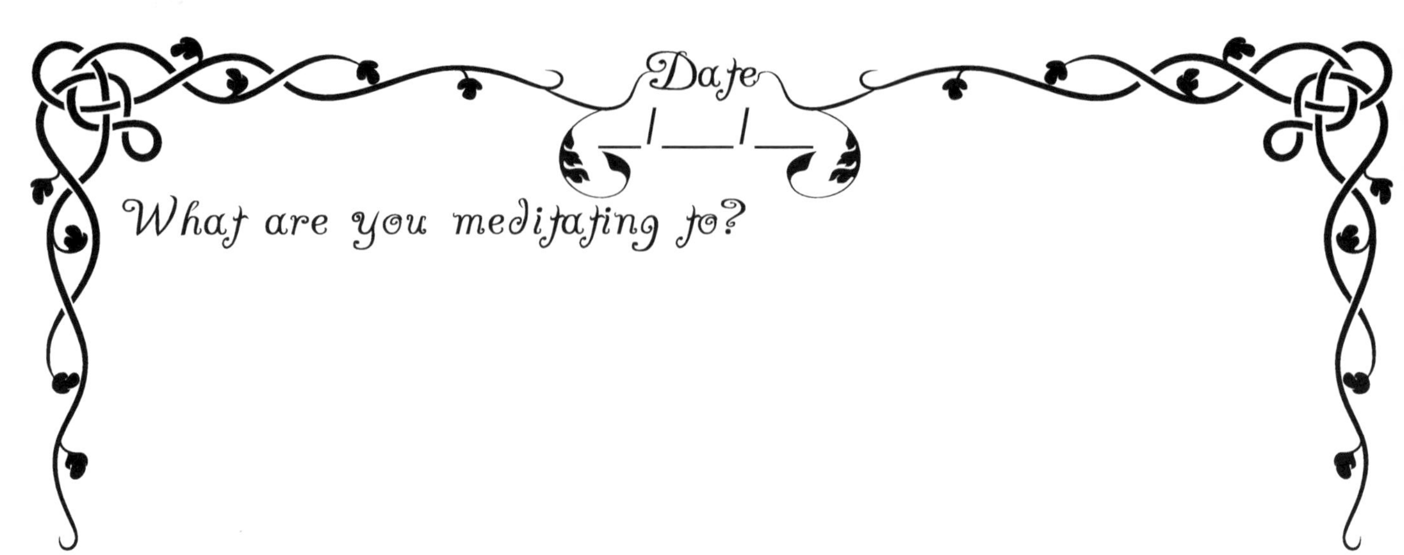

Date
__/__/__

What are you meditating to?

How do you feel before meditation?

What did you smell?

What did you hear?

What did you see?

Reflection.

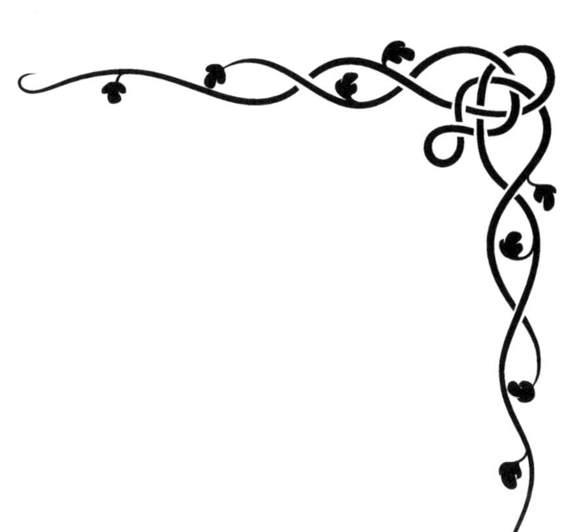

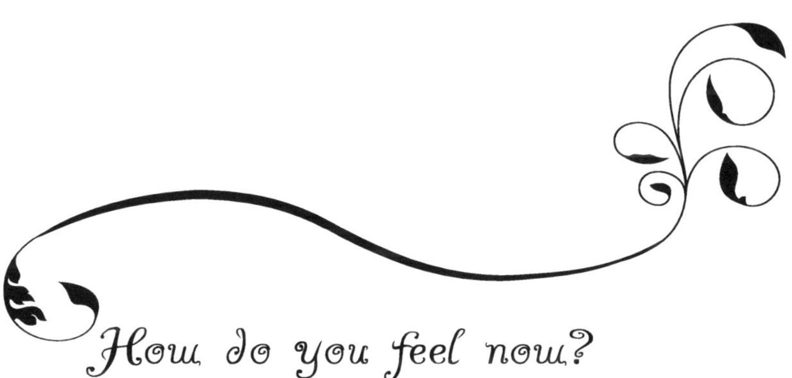

How do you feel now?

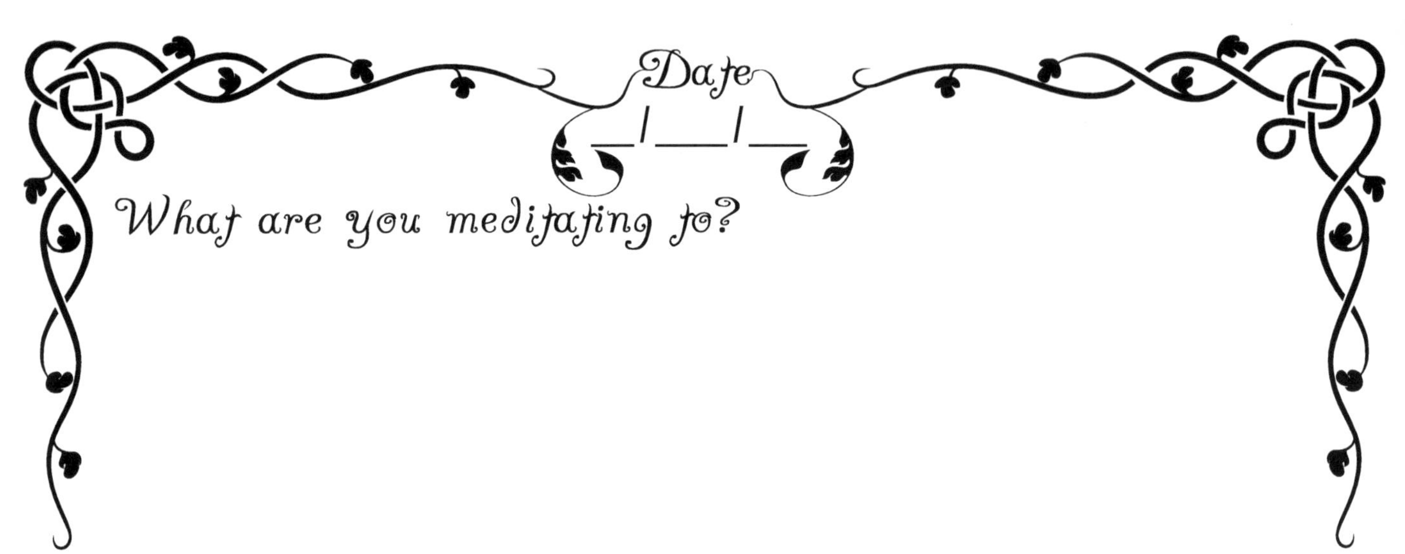

Date

__/____/____

What are you meditating to?

How do you feel before meditation?

What did you smell?

What did you hear?

What did you see?

Reflection.

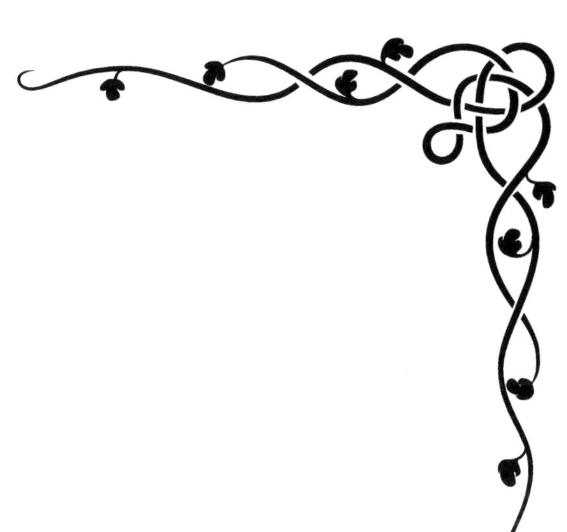

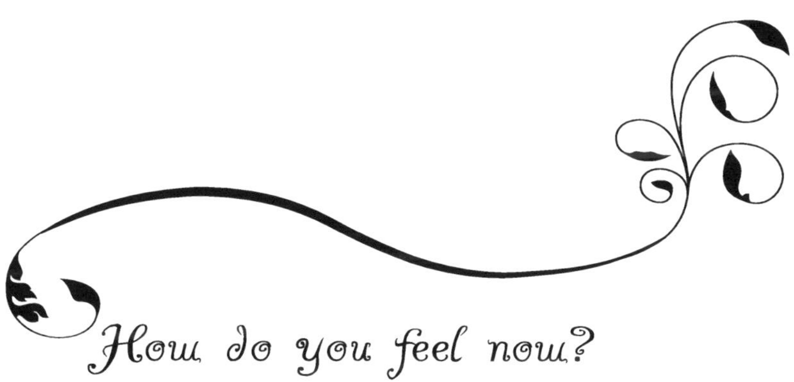

How do you feel now?

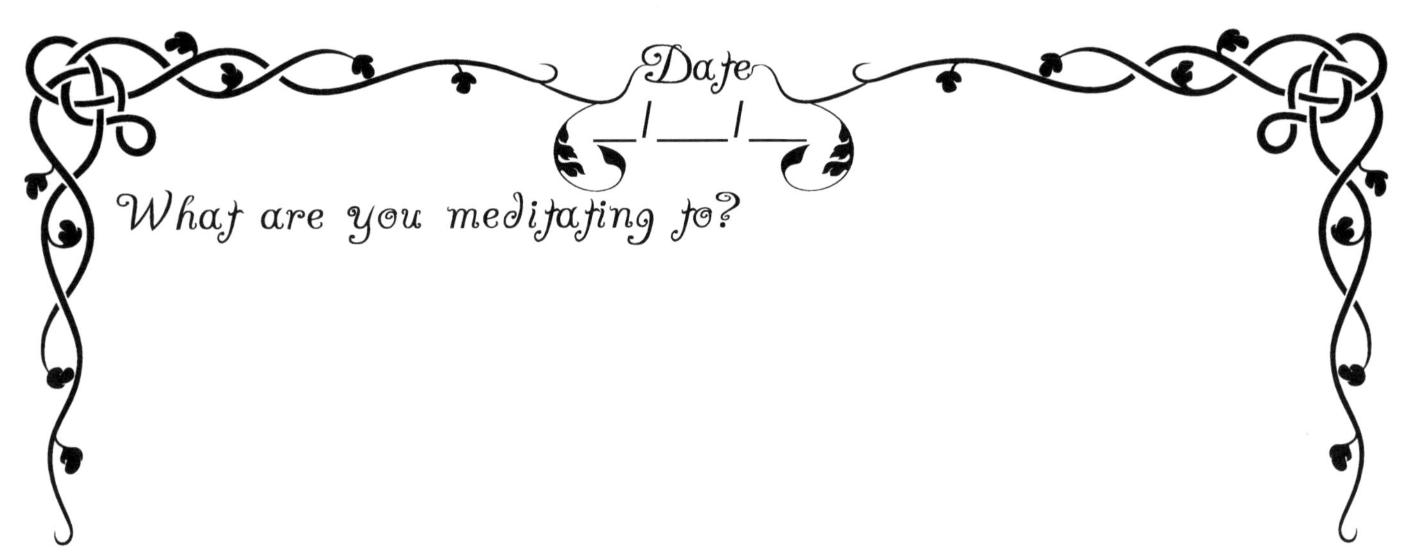

Date __/__/__

What are you meditating to?

How do you feel before meditation?

What did you smell?

What did you hear?

What did you see?

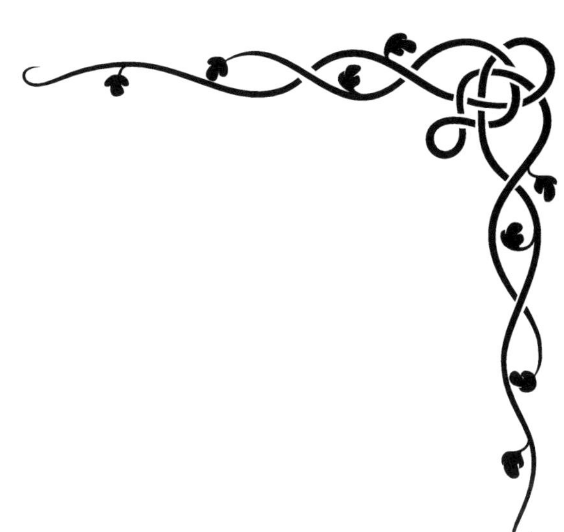

Reflection.

How do you feel now?

Date

__/__/__

What are you meditating to?

How do you feel before meditation?

What did you smell?

What did you hear?

What did you see?

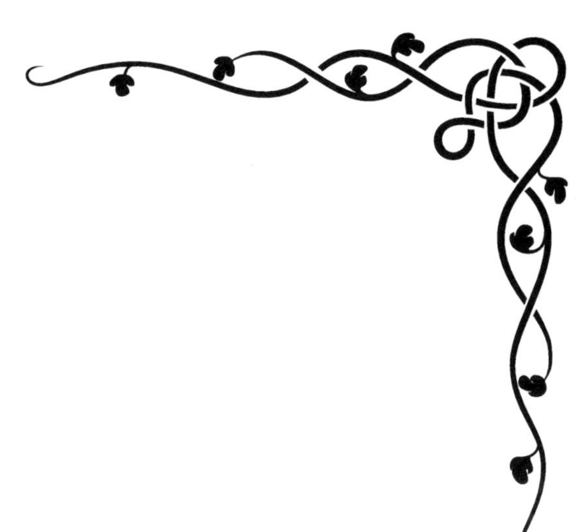

Reflection.

How do you feel now?

What are you meditating to?

How do you feel before meditation?

What did you smell?

What did you hear?

What did you see?

Reflection.

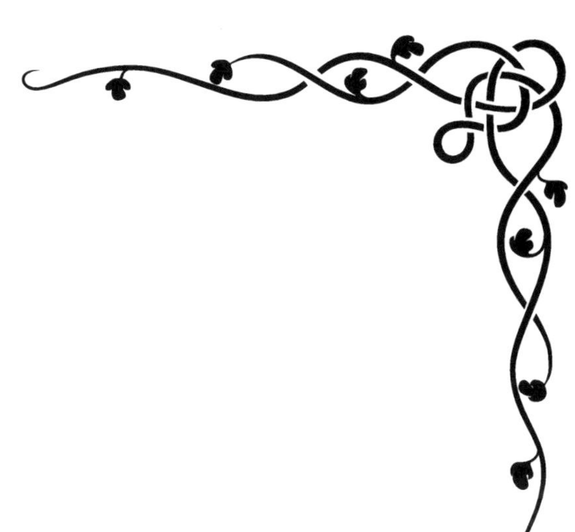

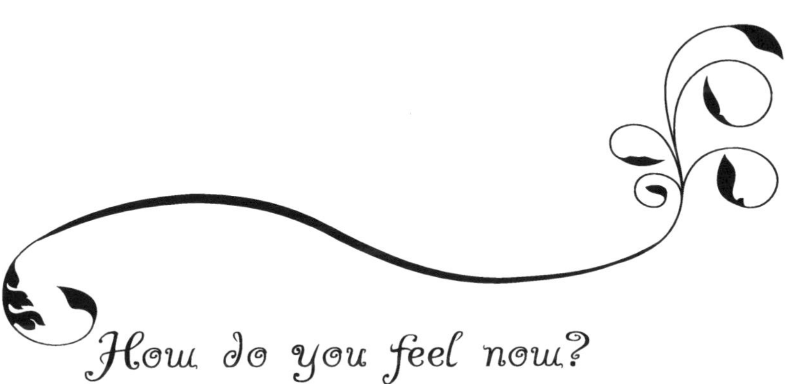

How do you feel now?

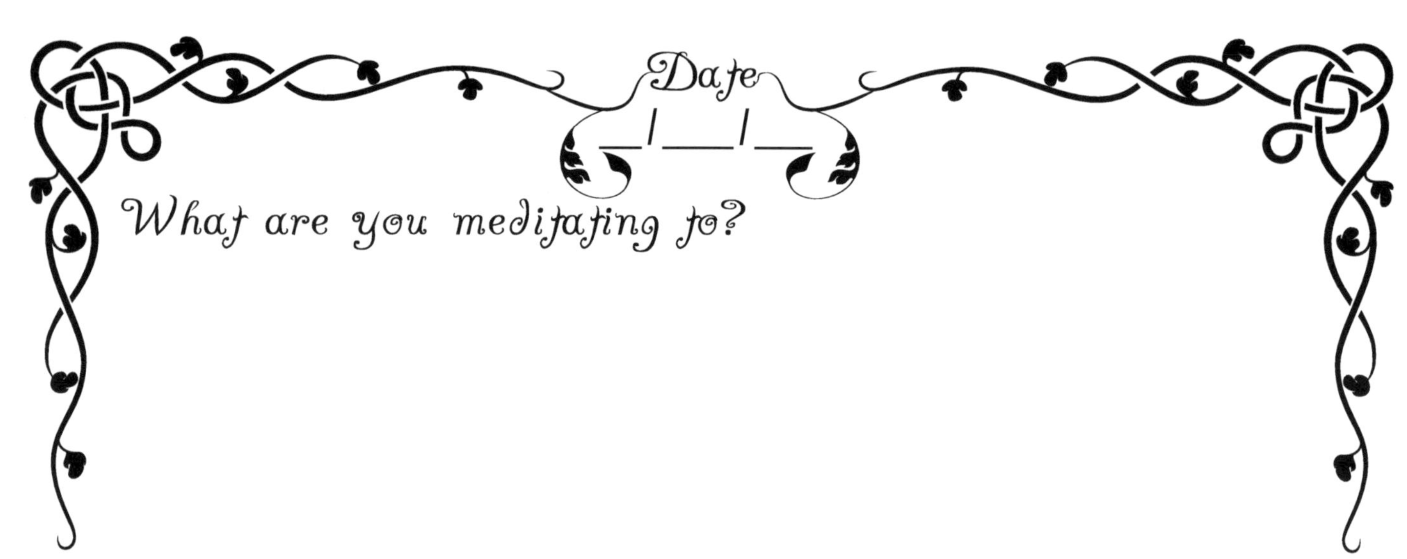

Date
__/____/____

What are you meditating to?

How do you feel before meditation?

What did you smell?

What did you hear?

What did you see?

Reflection.

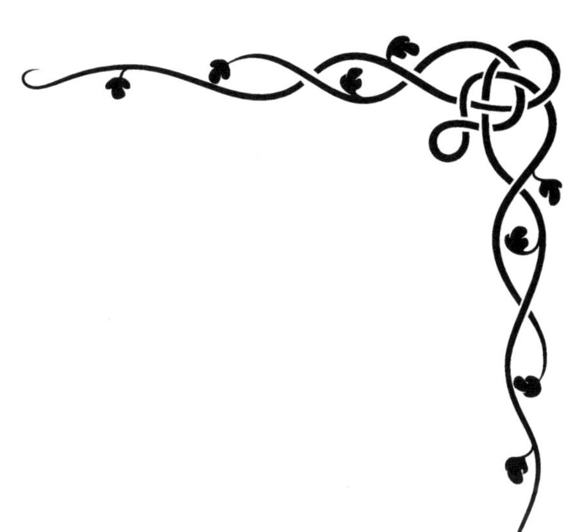

How do you feel now?

Date
__/__/__

What are you meditating to?

How do you feel before meditation?

What did you smell?

What did you hear?

What did you see?

Reflection.

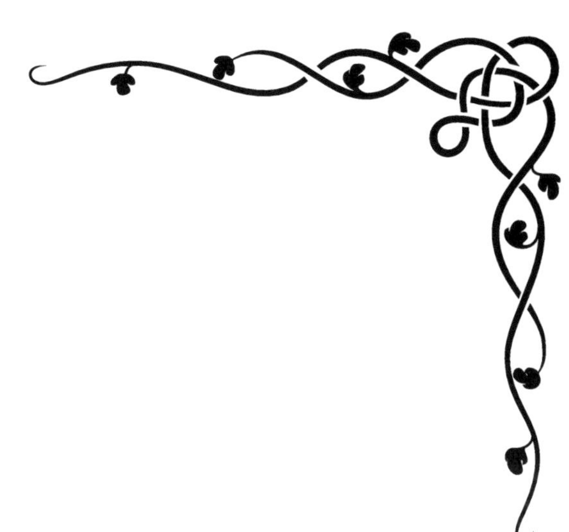

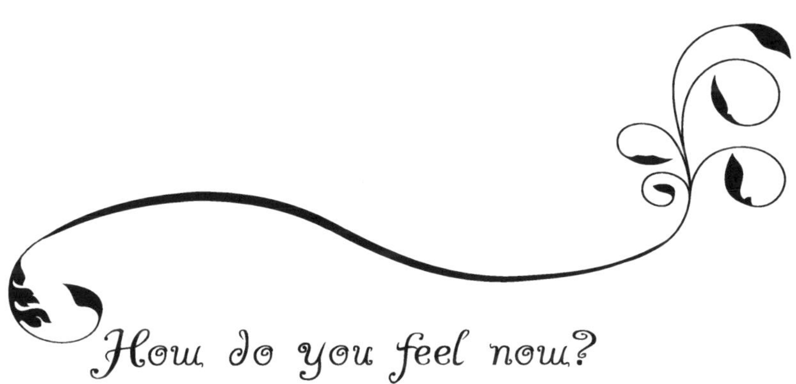

How do you feel now?

What are you meditating to?

How do you feel before meditation?

What did you smell?

What did you hear?

What did you see?

Reflection.

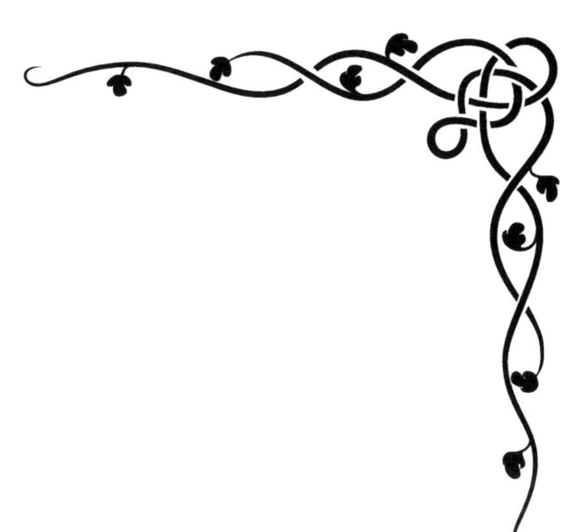

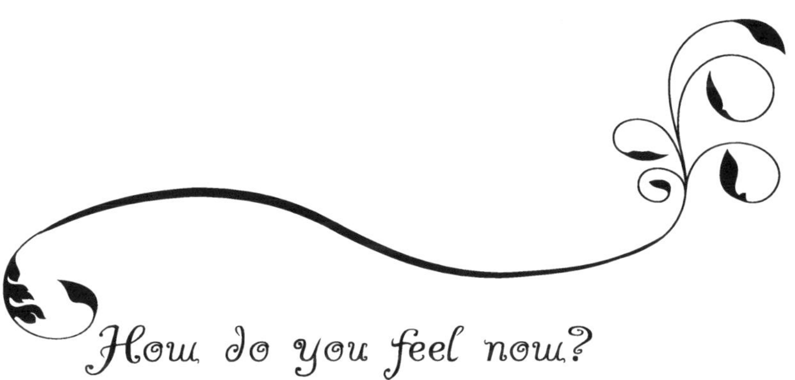

How do you feel now?

Date

__/__/__

What are you meditating to?

How do you feel before meditation?

What did you smell?

What did you hear?

What did you see?

Reflection.

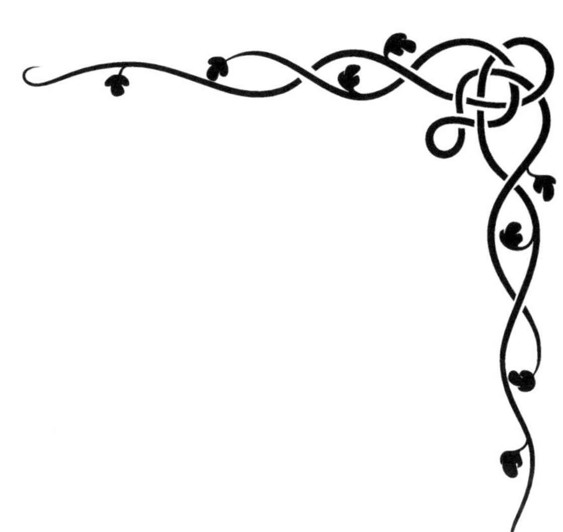

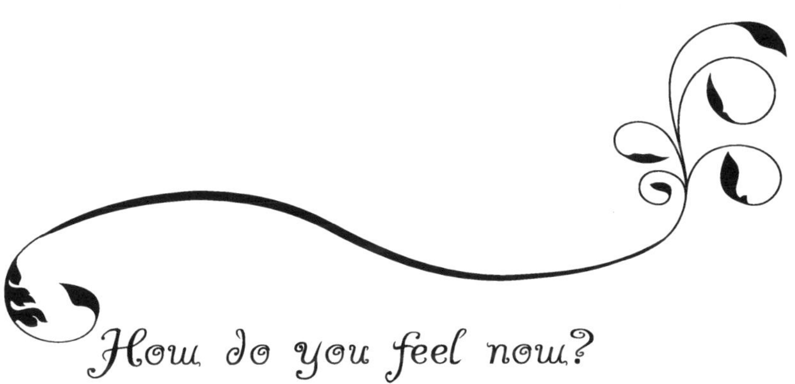

How do you feel now?

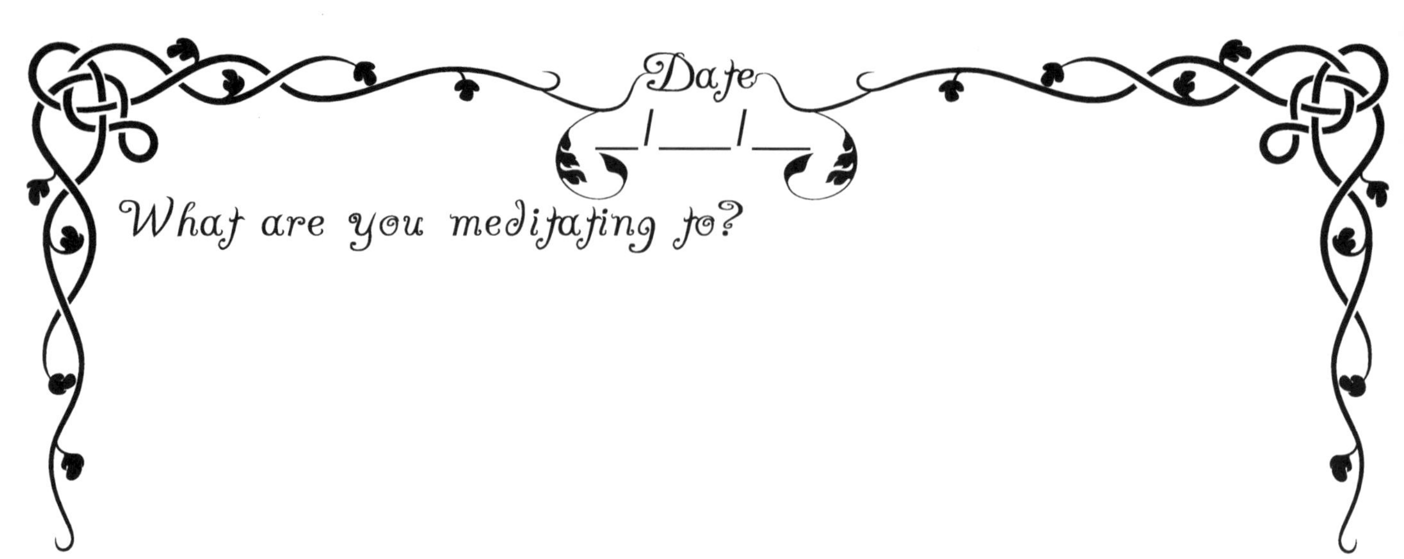

Date
__/__/__

What are you meditating to?

How do you feel before meditation?

What did you smell?

What did you hear?

What did you see?

Reflection.

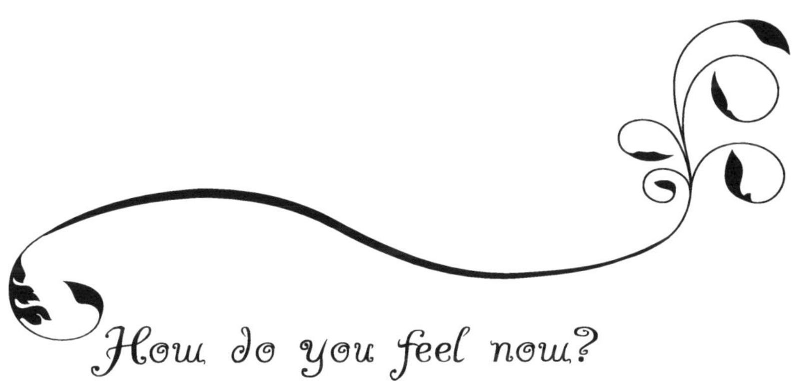

How do you feel now?

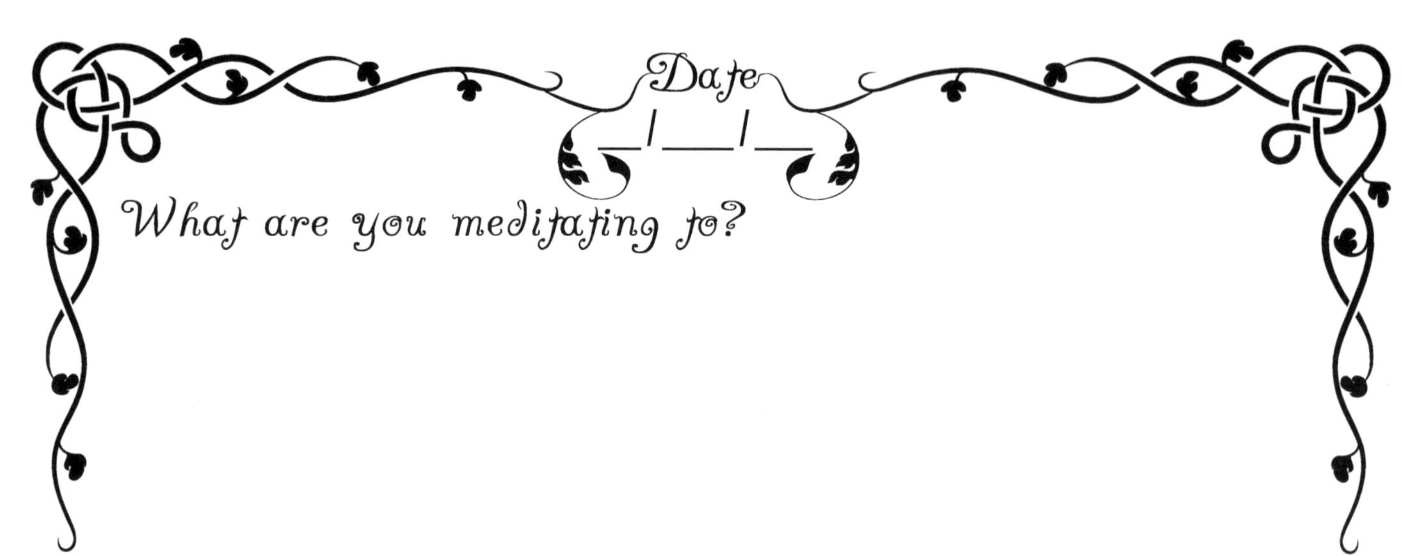

What are you meditating to?

How do you feel before meditation?

What did you smell?

What did you hear?

What did you see?

Reflection.

How do you feel now?

Date

__/__/__

What are you meditating to?

How do you feel before meditation?

What did you smell?

What did you hear?

What did you see?

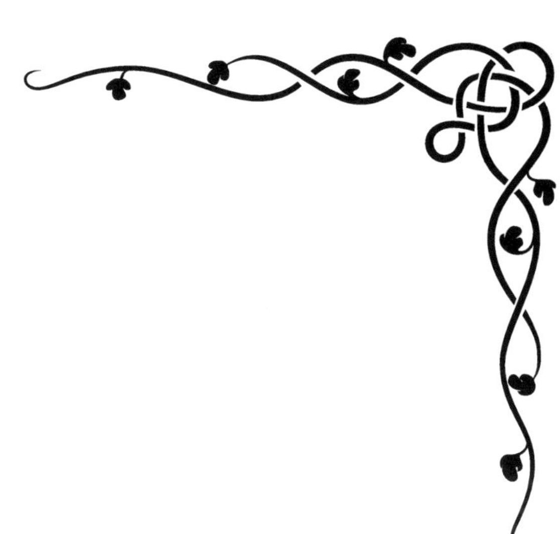

Reflection.

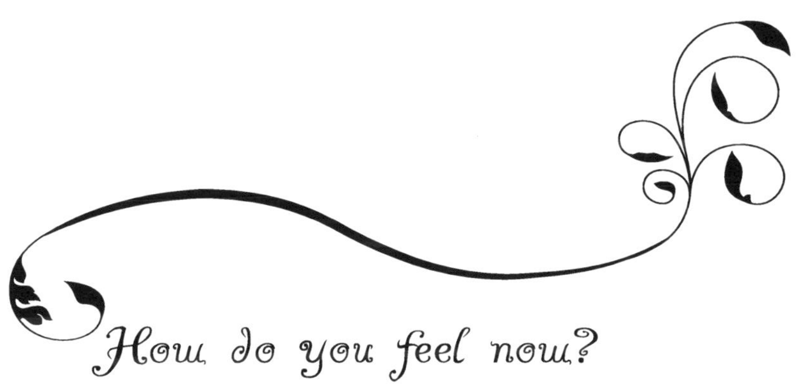

How do you feel now?

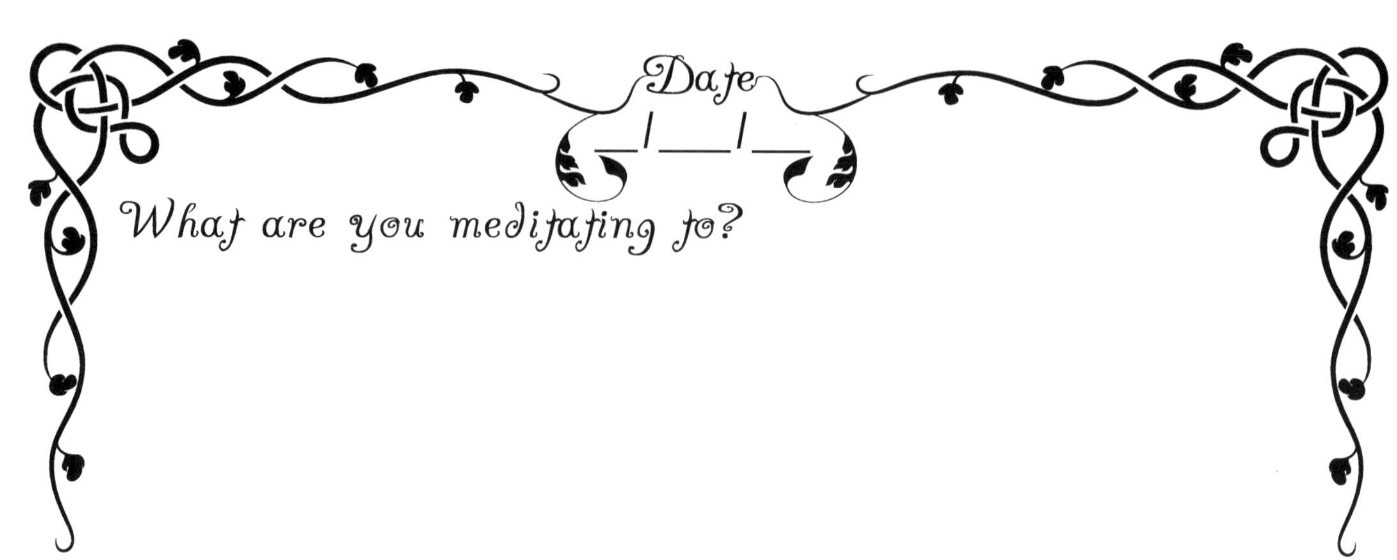

Date
__/__/__

What are you meditating to?

How do you feel before meditation?

What did you smell?

What did you hear?

What did you see?

Reflection.

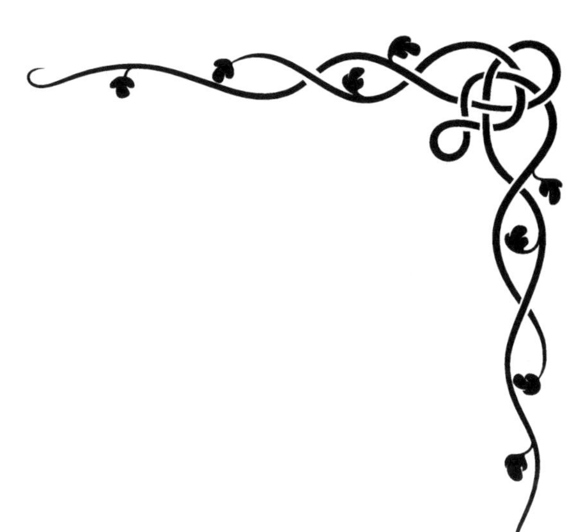

How do you feel now?

What are you meditating to?

How do you feel before meditation?

What did you smell?

What did you hear?

What did you see?

Reflection.

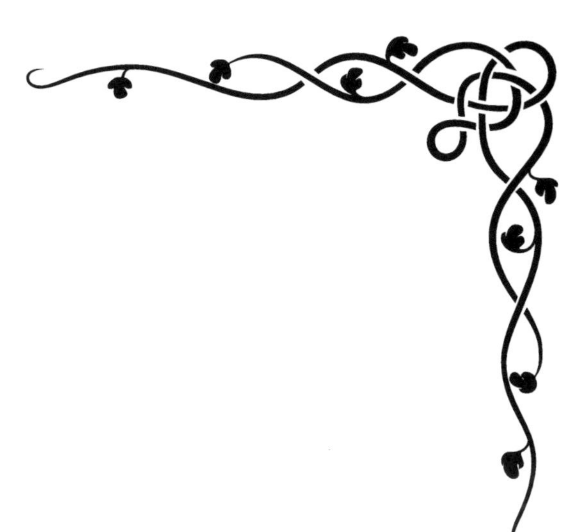

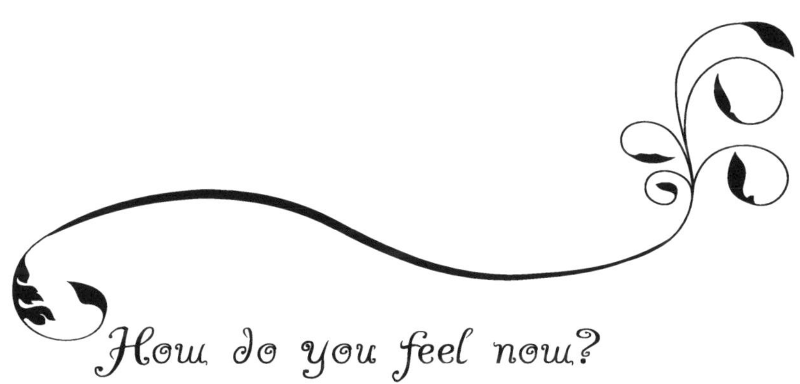

How do you feel now?

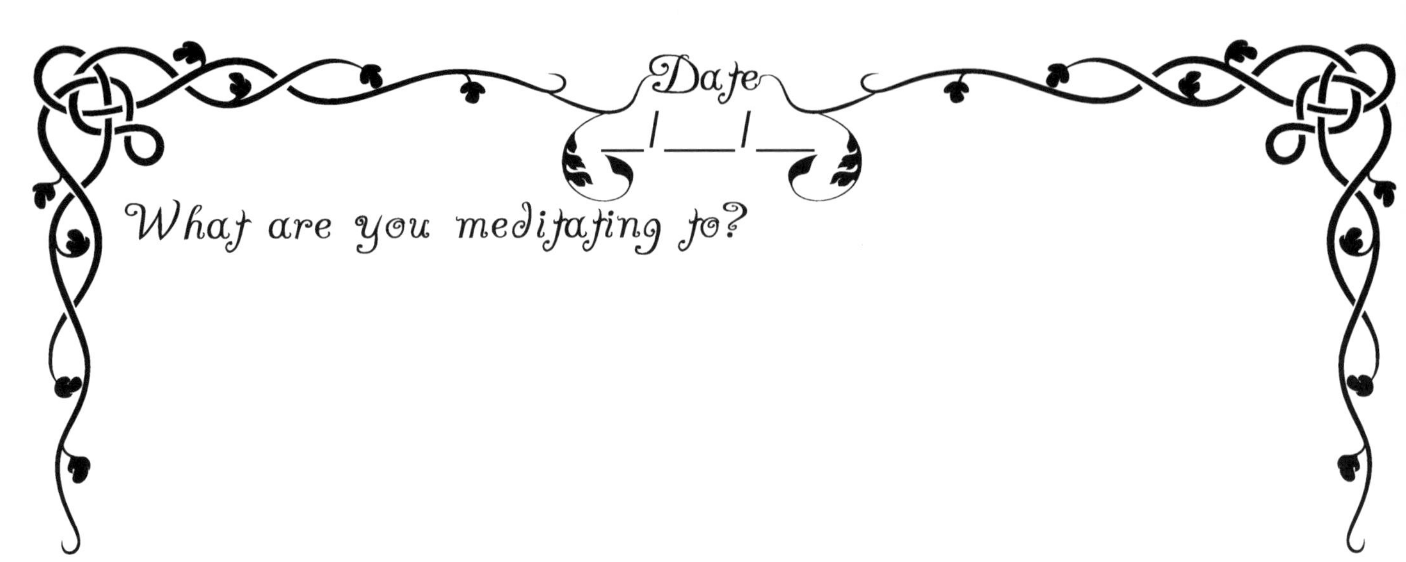

Date

__/__/__

What are you meditating to?

How do you feel before meditation?

What did you smell?

What did you hear?

What did you see?

Reflection.

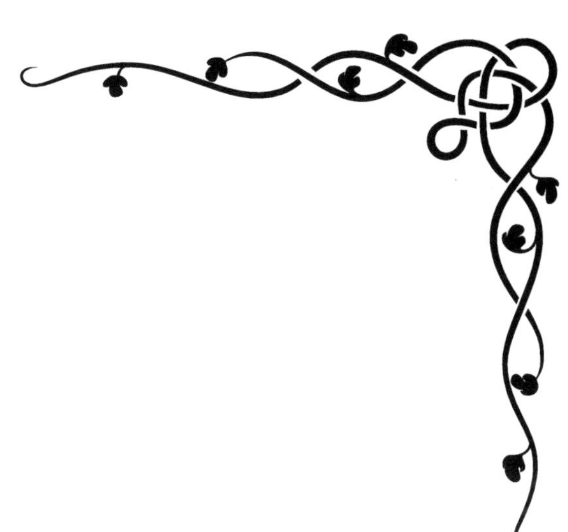

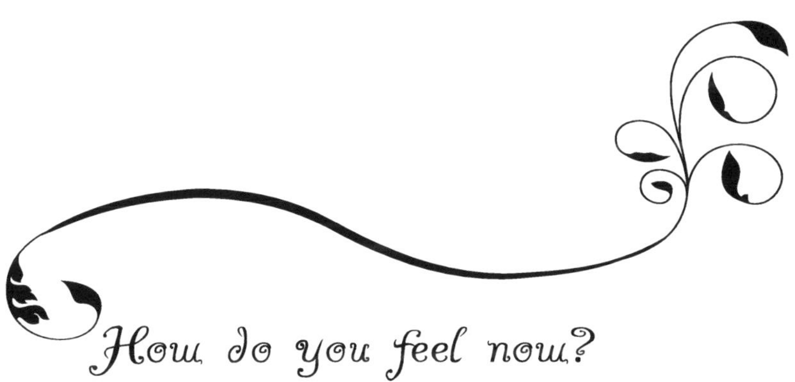

How do you feel now?

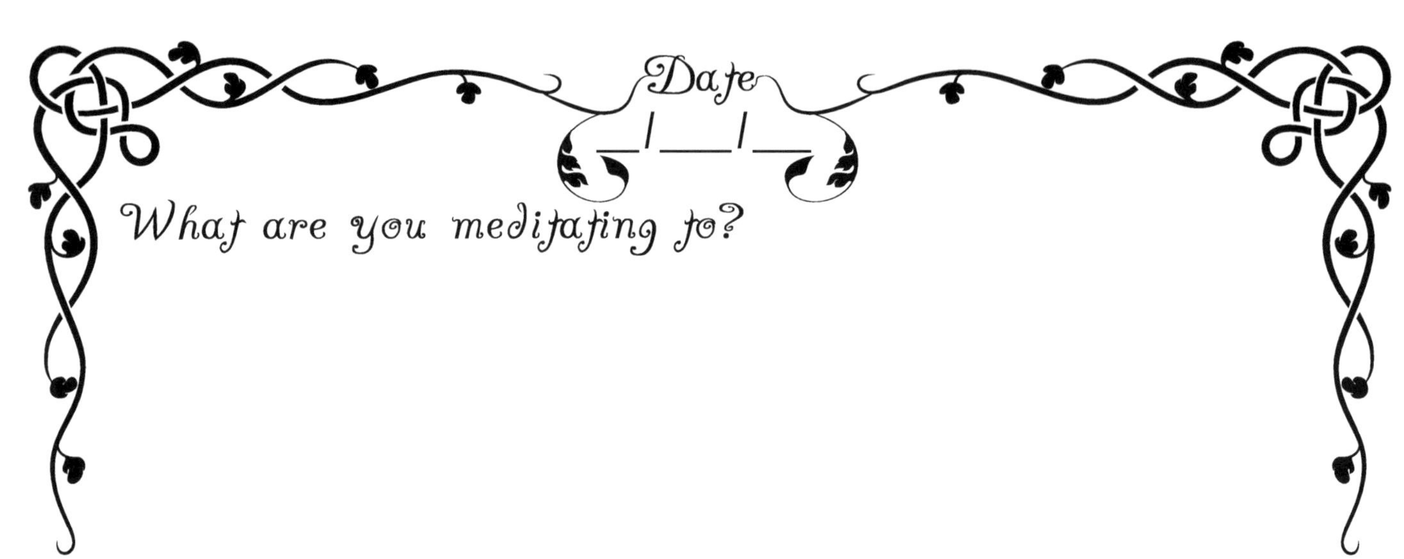

What are you meditating to?

How do you feel before meditation?

What did you smell?

What did you hear?

What did you see?

Reflection.

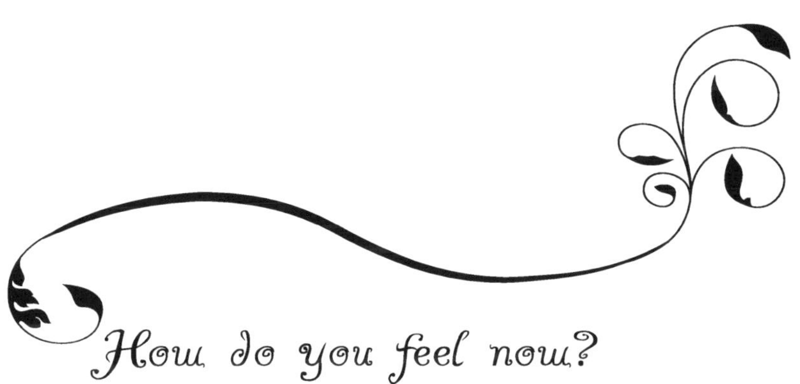

How do you feel now?

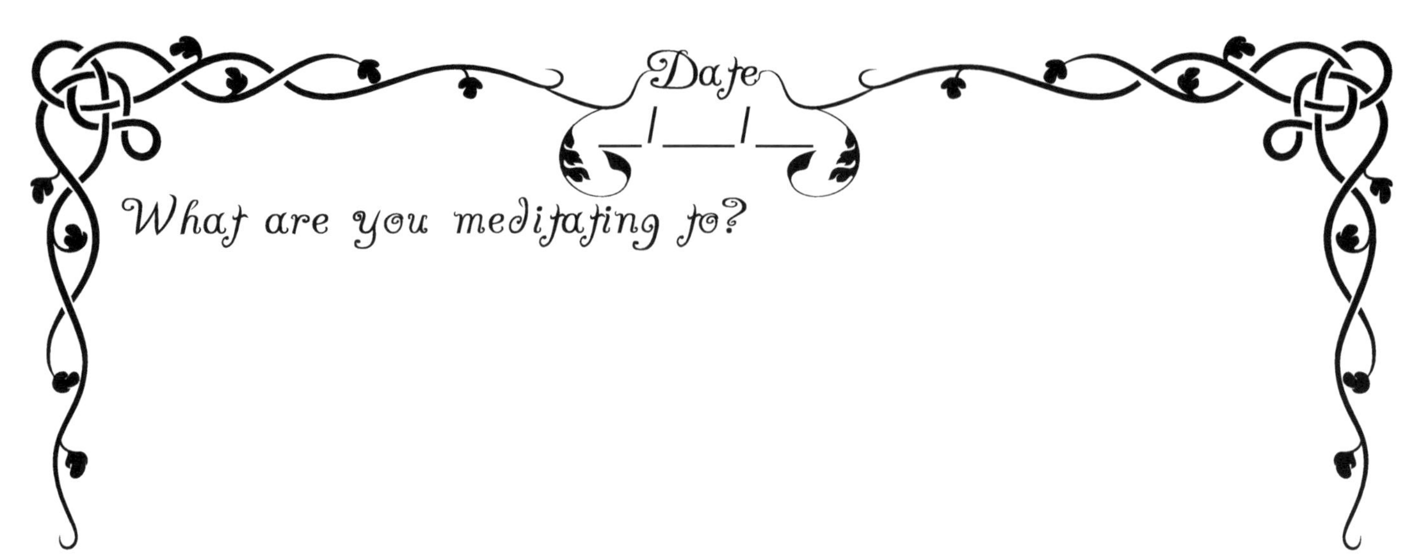

Date

__/__/__

What are you meditating to?

How do you feel before meditation?

What did you smell?

What did you hear?

What did you see?

Reflection.

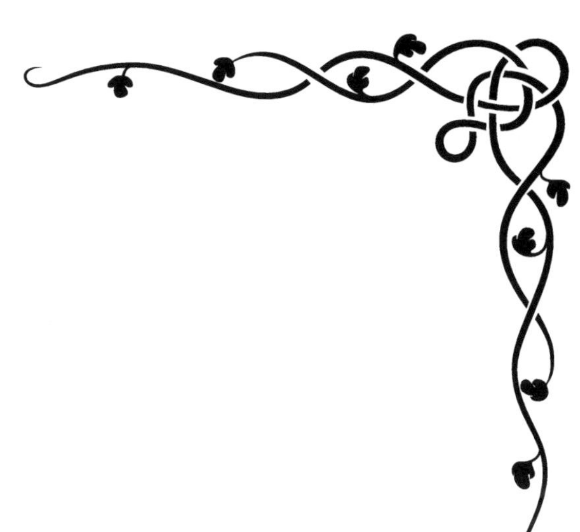

How do you feel now?

Date __/__/__

What are you meditating to?

How do you feel before meditation?

What did you smell?

What did you hear?

What did you see?

Reflection.

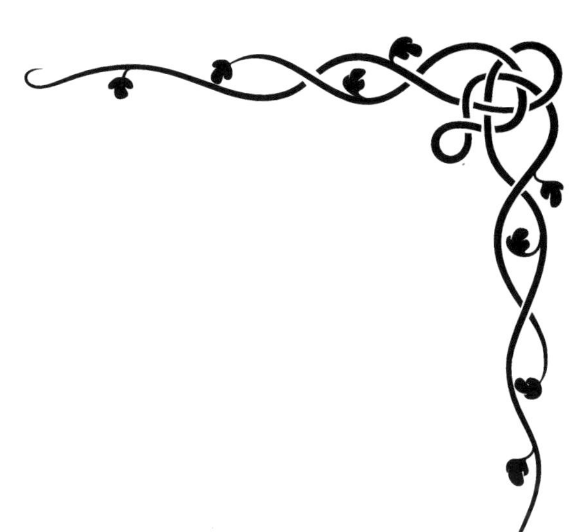

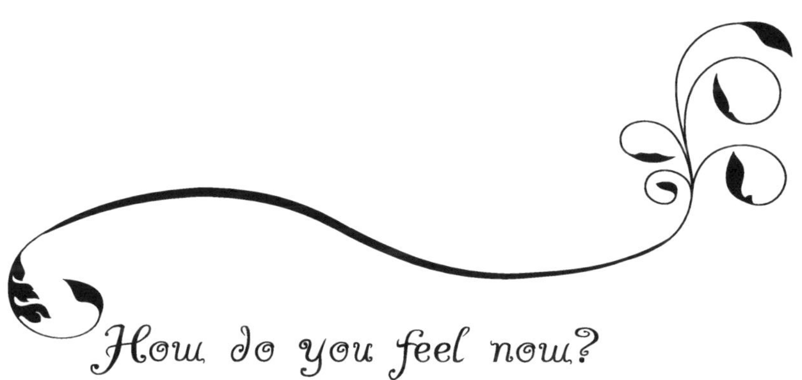

How do you feel now?

What are you meditating to?

How do you feel before meditation?

What did you smell?

What did you hear?

What did you see?

Reflection.

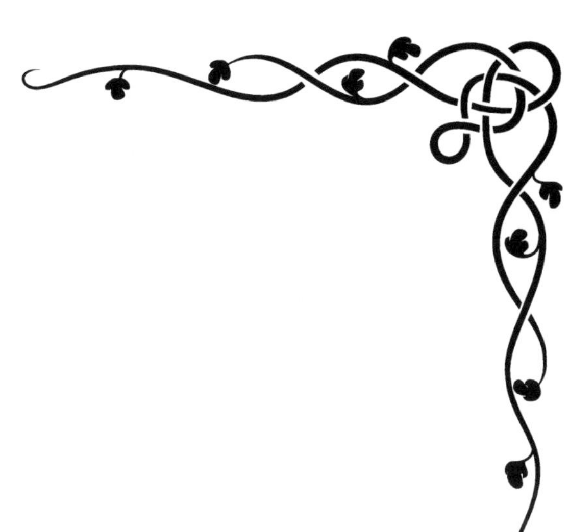

How do you feel now?

Date
__/__/__

What are you meditating to?

How do you feel before meditation?

What did you smell?

What did you hear?

What did you see?

Reflection.

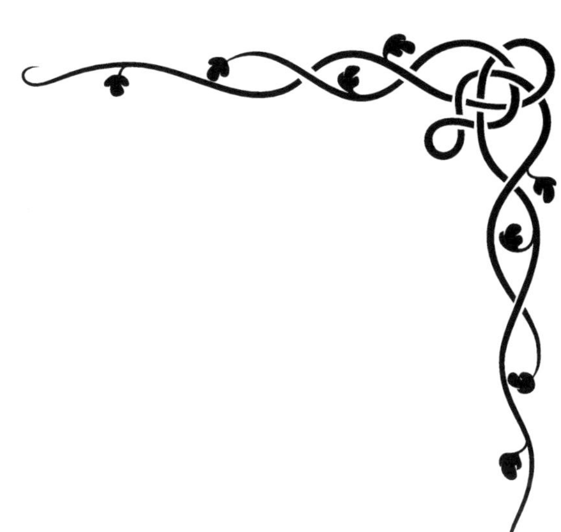

How do you feel now?

What are you meditating to?

How do you feel before meditation?

What did you smell?

What did you hear?

What did you see?

Reflection.

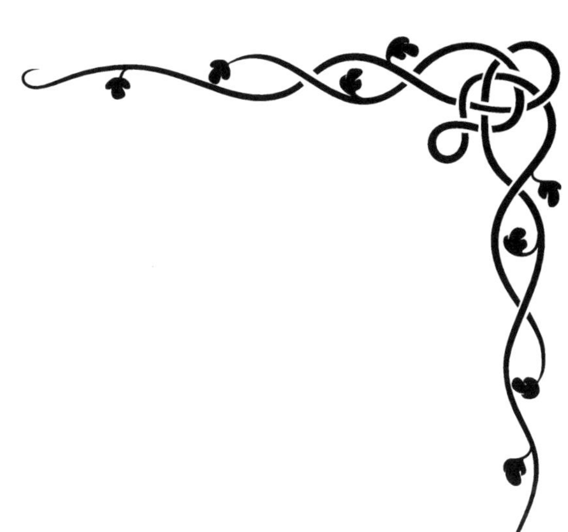

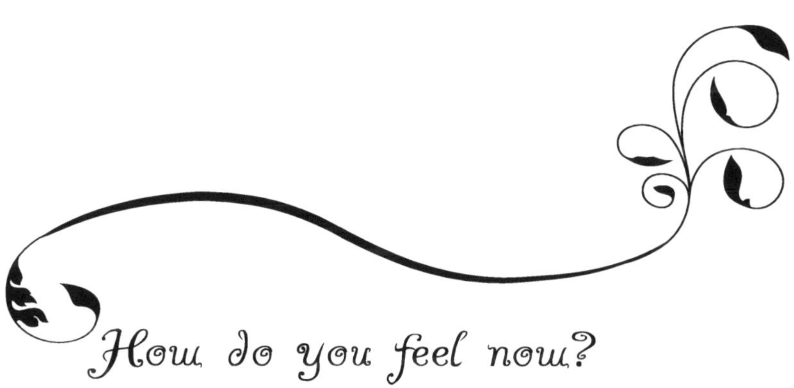

How do you feel now?

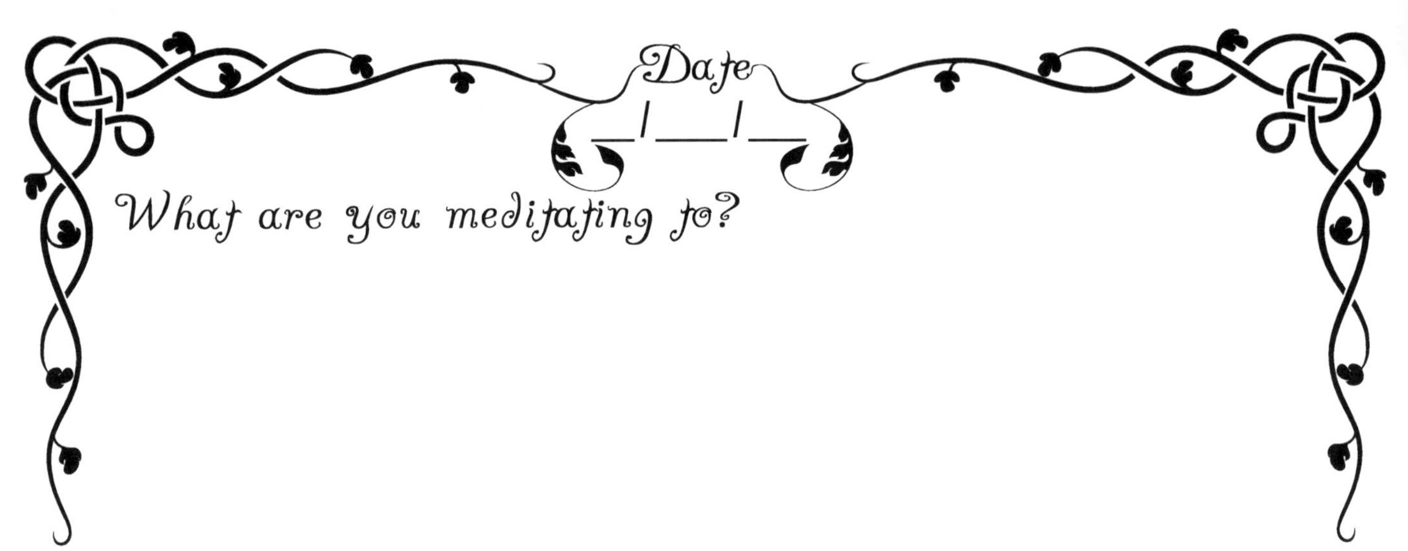

Date
__/__/__

What are you meditating to?

How do you feel before meditation?

What did you smell?

What did you hear?

What did you see?

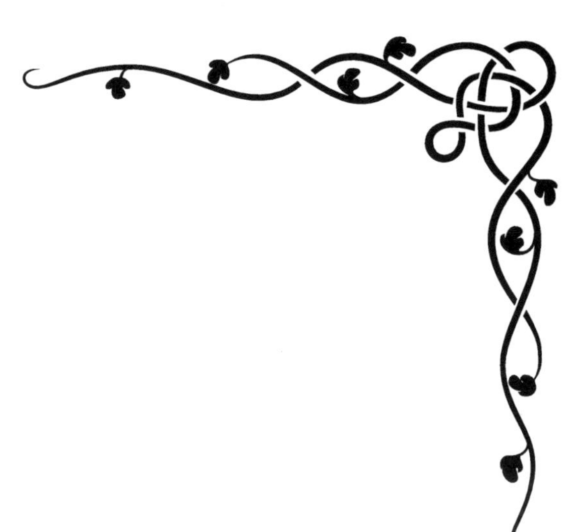

Reflection.

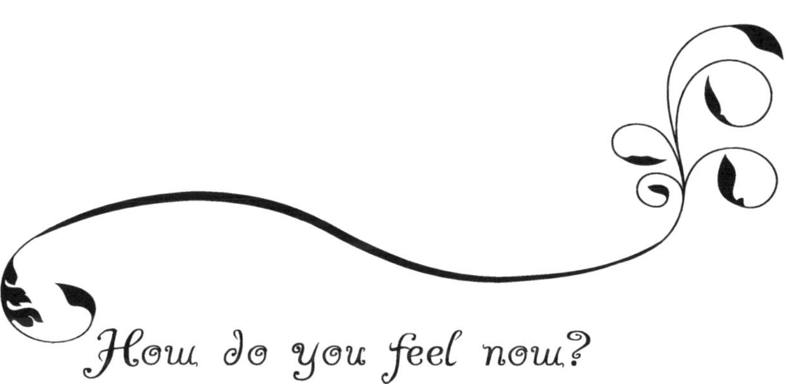

How do you feel now?

What are you meditating to?

How do you feel before meditation?

What did you smell?

What did you hear?

What did you see?

Reflection.

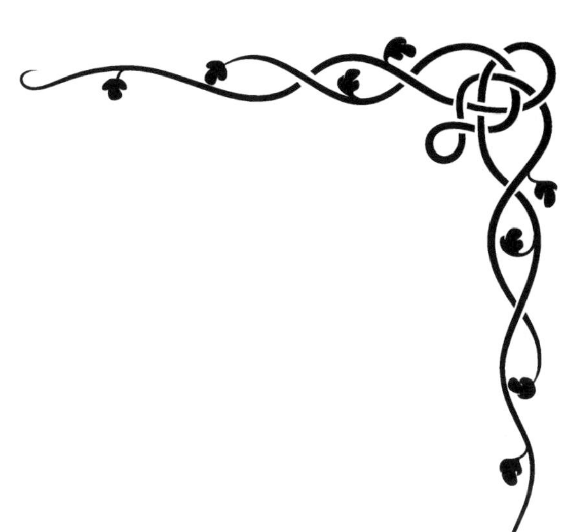

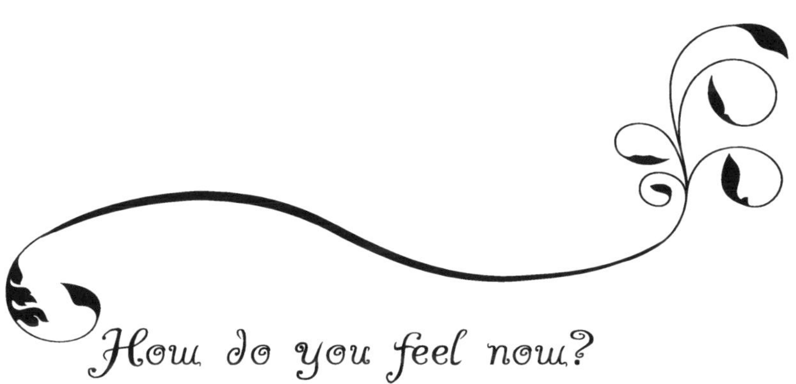

How do you feel now?

Date
__/__/__

What are you meditating to?

How do you feel before meditation?

What did you smell?

What did you hear?

What did you see?

Reflection.

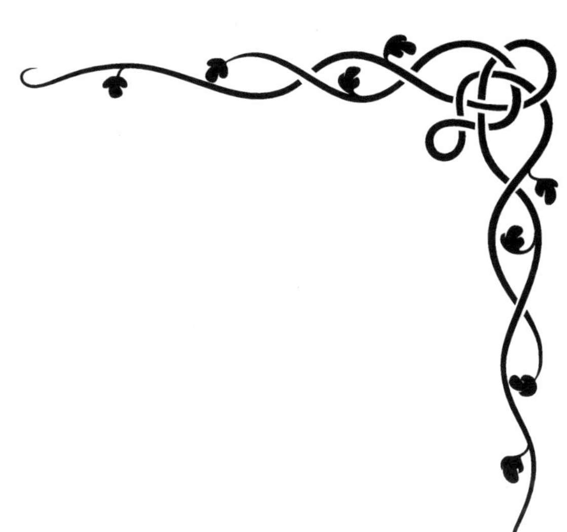

How do you feel now?

Date __/__/__

What are you meditating to?

How do you feel before meditation?

What did you smell?

What did you hear?

What did you see?

Reflection.

How do you feel now?

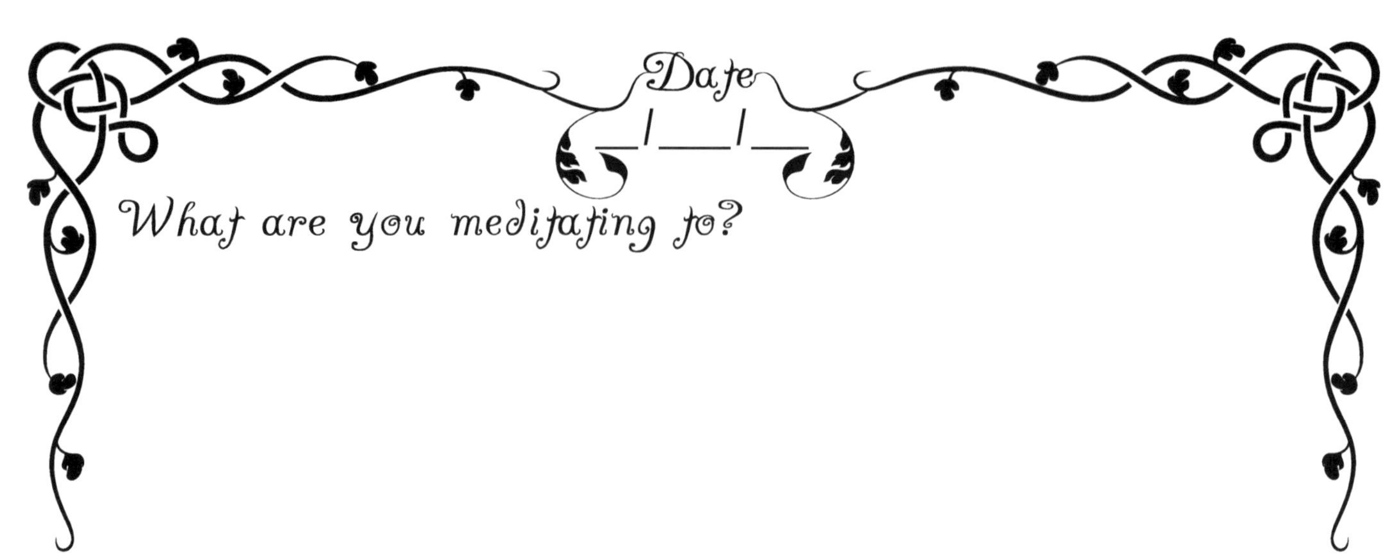

Date

__/__/__

What are you meditating to?

How do you feel before meditation?

What did you smell?

What did you hear?

What did you see?

Reflection.

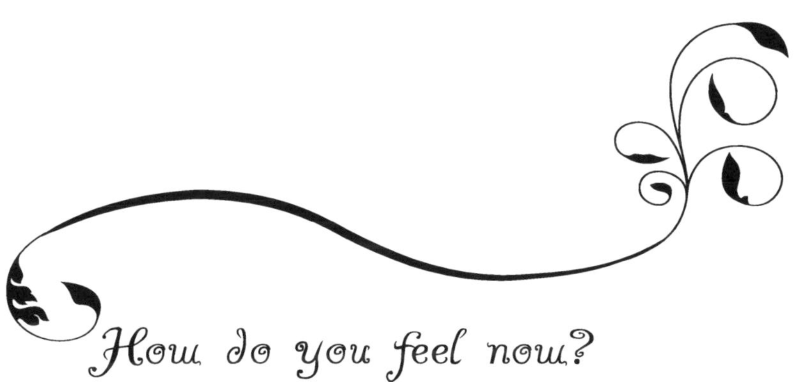

How do you feel now?

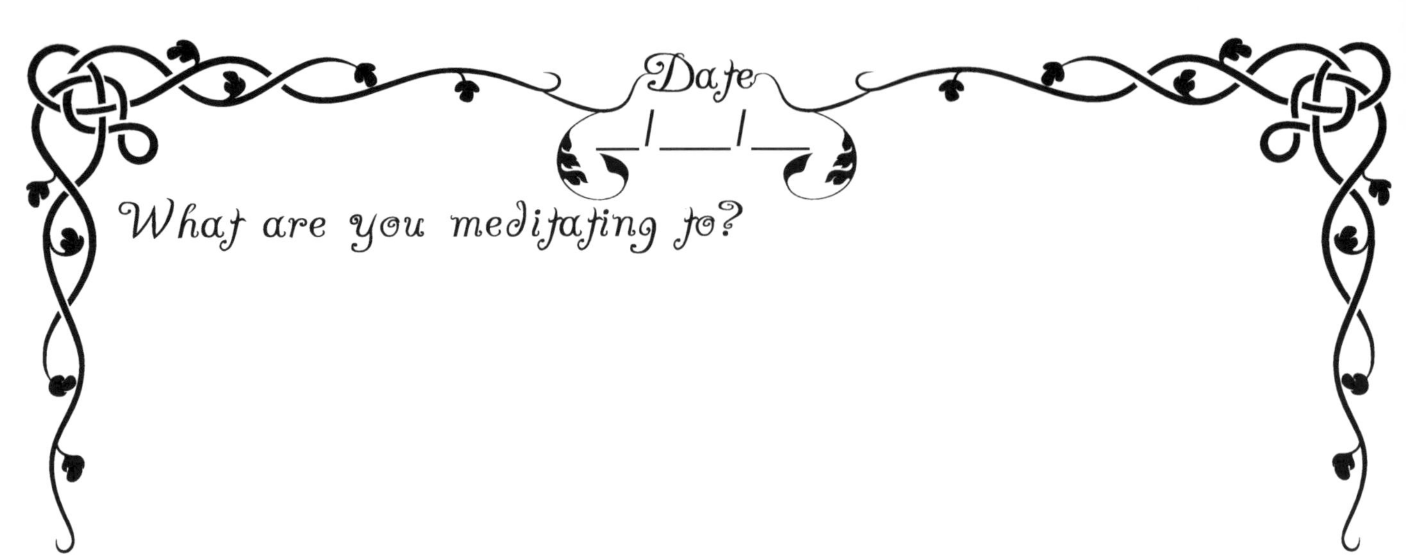

What are you meditating to?

How do you feel before meditation?

What did you smell?

What did you hear?

What did you see?

Reflection.

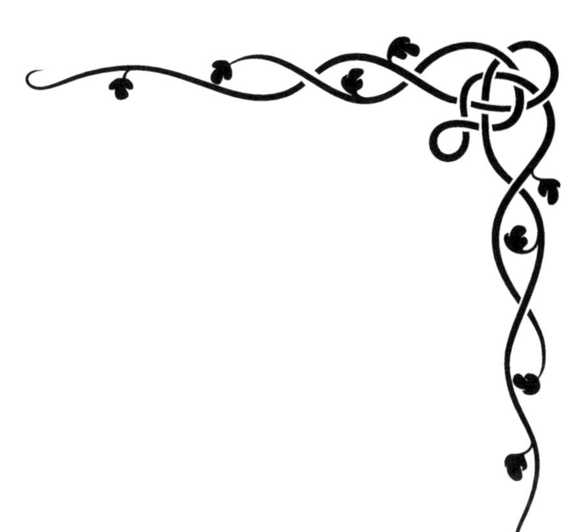

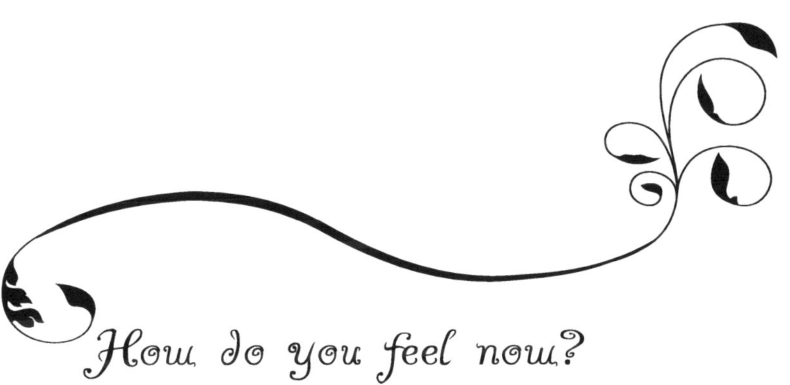

How do you feel now?

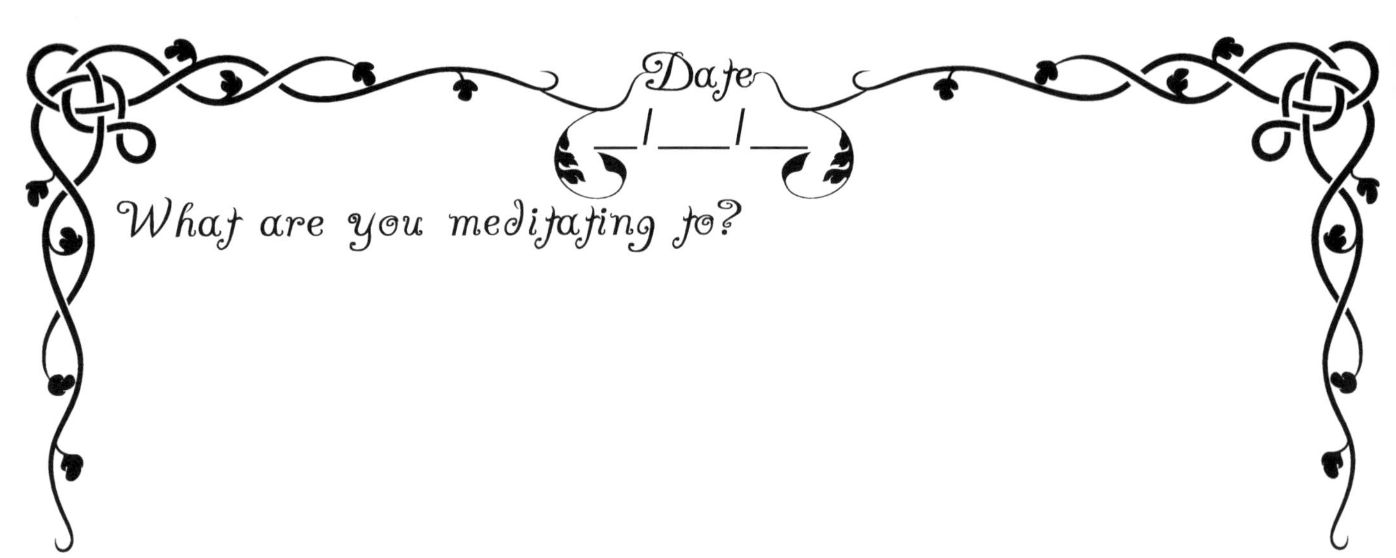

Date

__/___/__

What are you meditating to?

How do you feel before meditation?

What did you smell?

What did you hear?

What did you see?

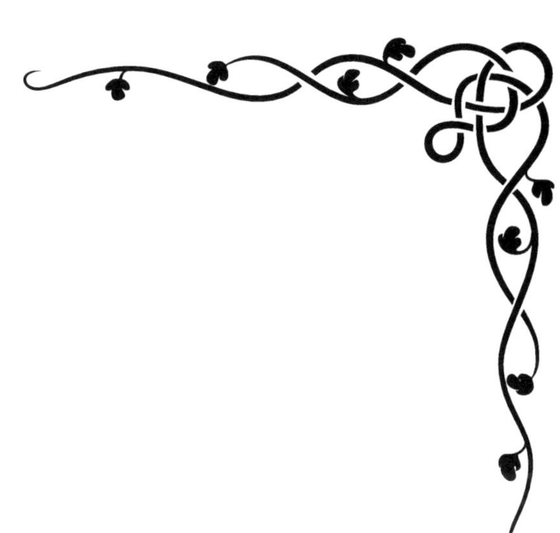

Reflection.

How do you feel now?

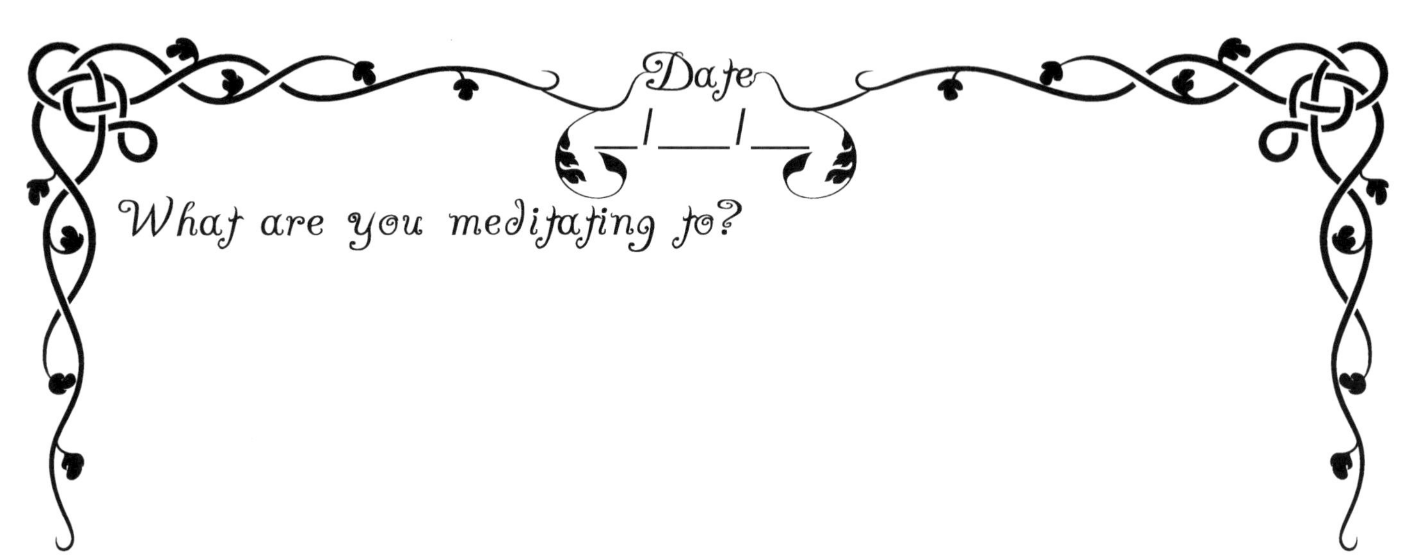

What are you meditating to?

How do you feel before meditation?

What did you smell?

What did you hear?

What did you see?

Reflection.

How do you feel now?

Date

__/__/__

What are you meditating to?

How do you feel before meditation?

What did you smell?

What did you hear?

What did you see?

Reflection.

How do you feel now?

What are you meditating to?

How do you feel before meditation?

What did you smell?

What did you hear?

What did you see?

Reflection.

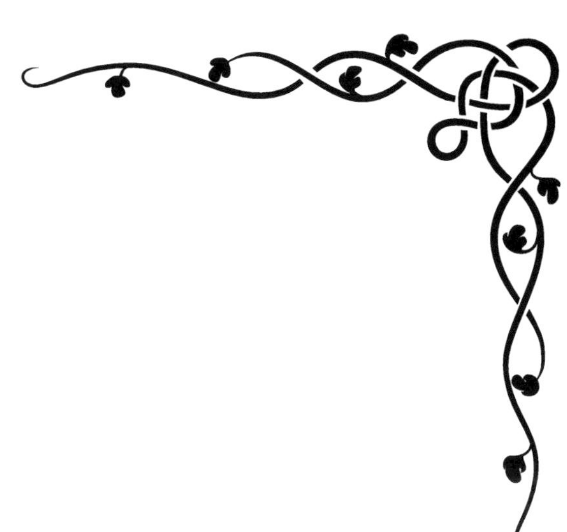

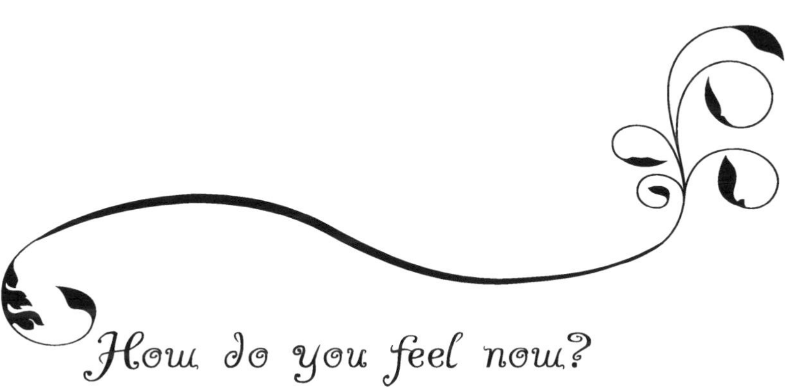

How do you feel now?

Date

__/__/__

What are you meditating to?

How do you feel before meditation?

What did you smell?

What did you hear?

What did you see?

Reflection.

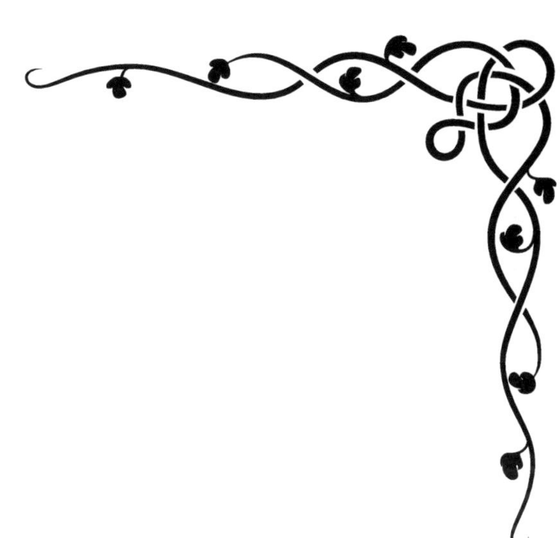

How do you feel now?

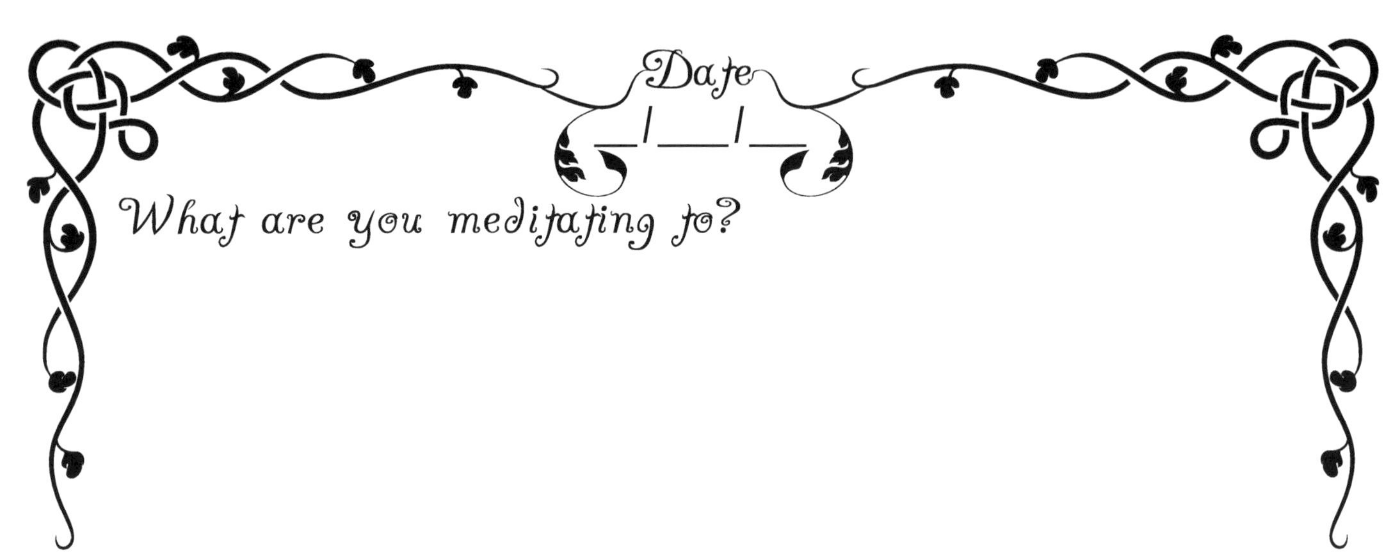

Date

__/___/___

What are you meditating to?

How do you feel before meditation?

What did you smell?

What did you hear?

What did you see?

Reflection.

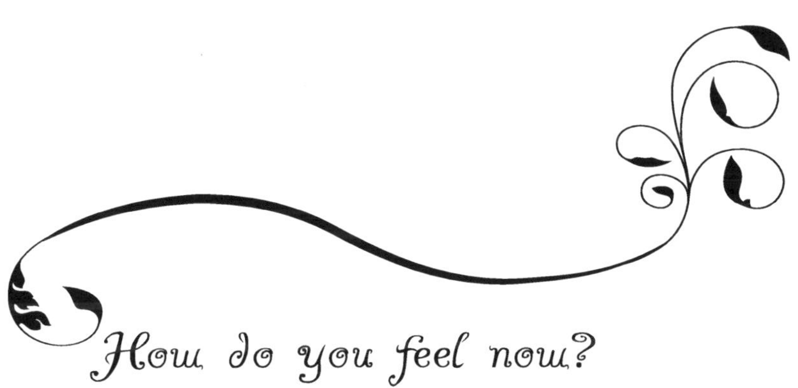

How do you feel now?

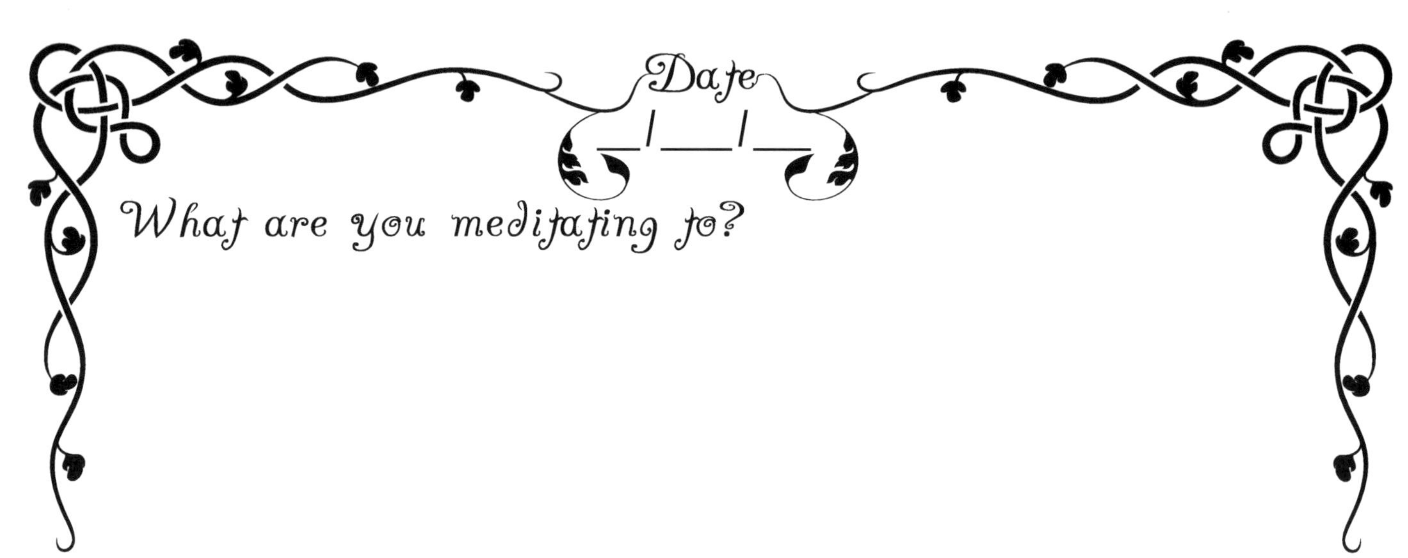

What are you meditating to?

How do you feel before meditation?

What did you smell?

What did you hear?

What did you see?

Reflection.

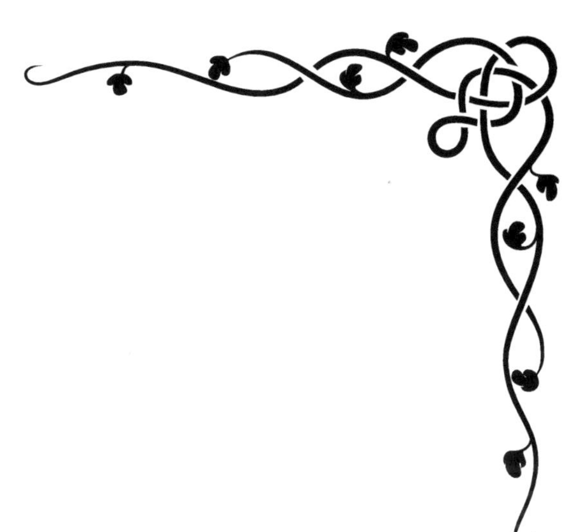

How do you feel now?

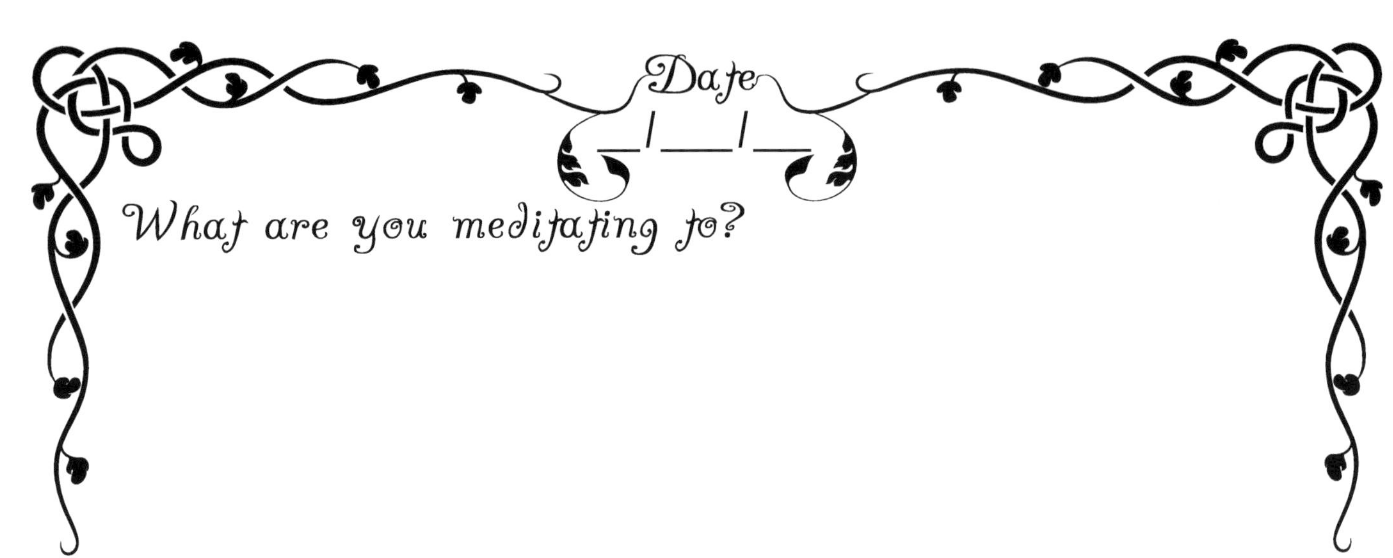

Date

__/____/__

What are you meditating to?

How do you feel before meditation?

What did you smell?

What did you hear?

What did you see?

Reflection.

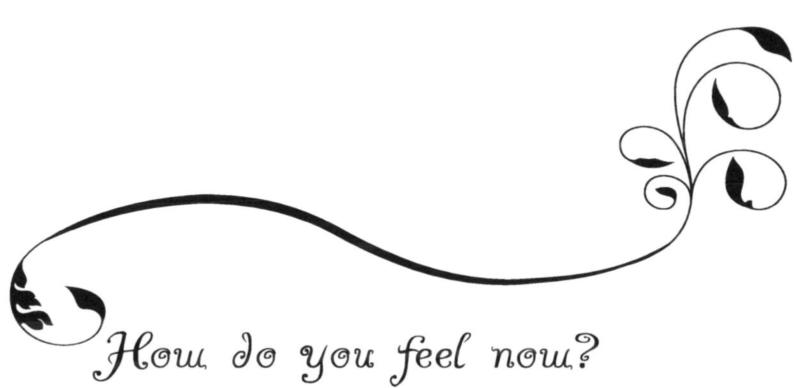

How do you feel now?

Date

__/__/__

What are you meditating to?

How do you feel before meditation?

What did you smell?

What did you hear?

What did you see?

Reflection.

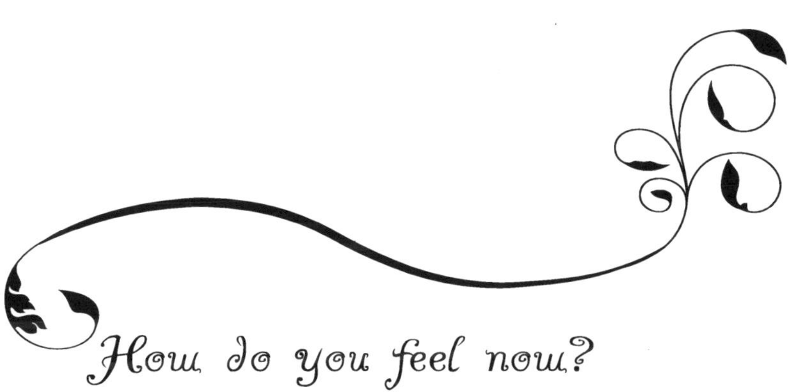

How do you feel now?

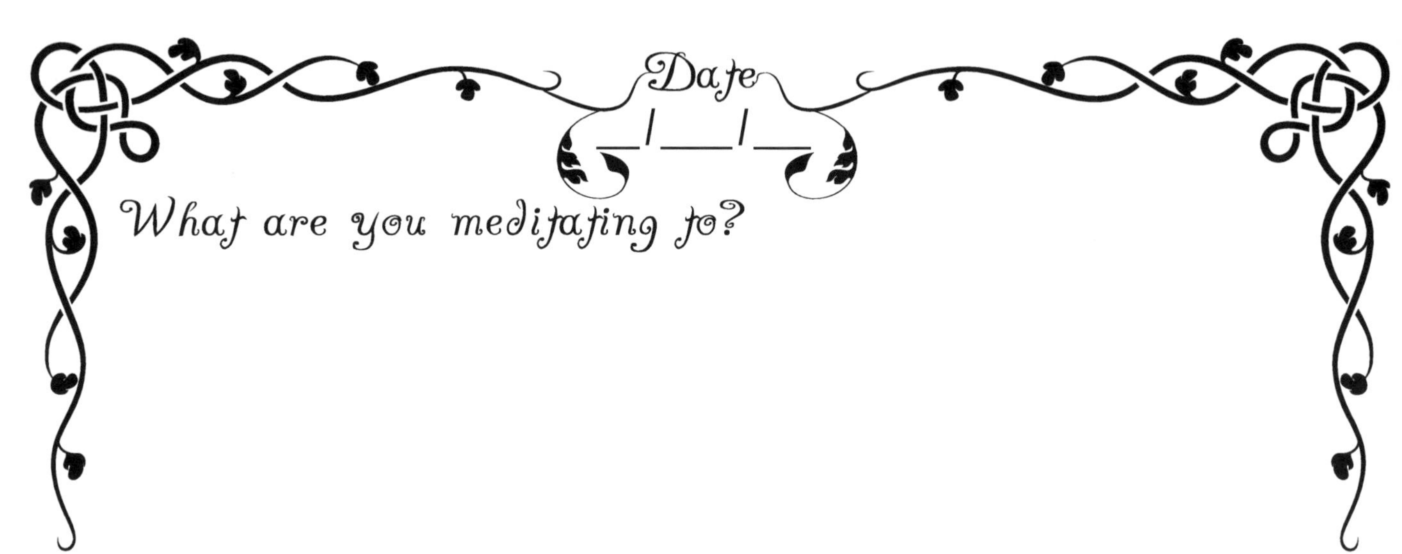

What are you meditating to?

How do you feel before meditation?

What did you smell?

What did you hear?

What did you see?

Reflection.

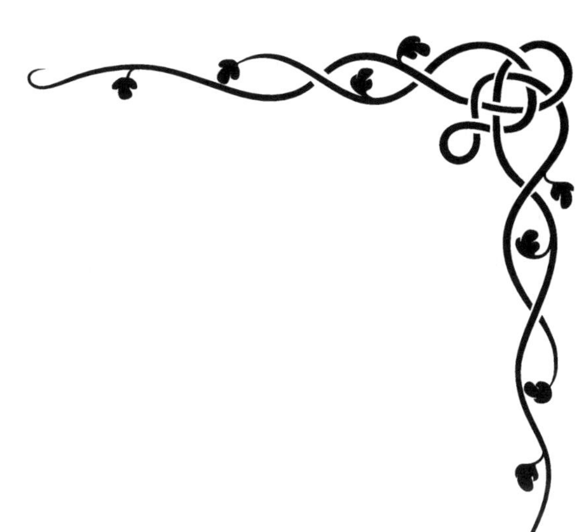

How do you feel now?

Date

__/__/__

What are you meditating to?

How do you feel before meditation?

What did you smell?

What did you hear?

What did you see?

Reflection.

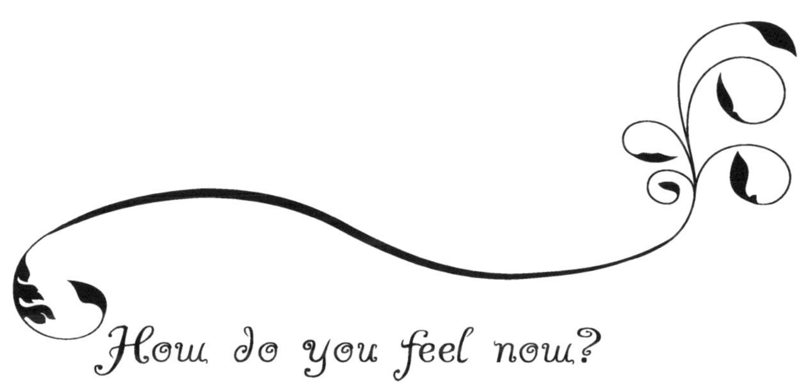

How do you feel now?

Date
__/___/__

What are you meditating to?

How do you feel before meditation?

What did you smell?

What did you hear?

What did you see?

Reflection.

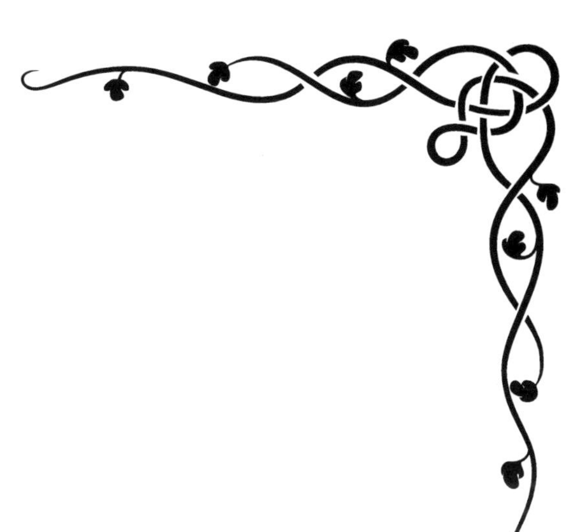

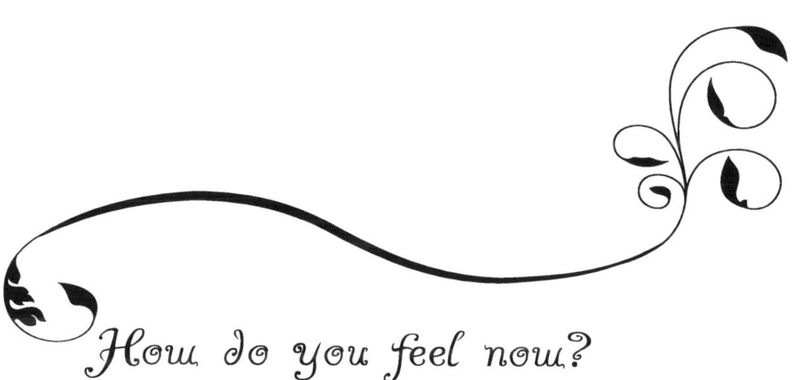

How do you feel now?

What are you meditating to?

How do you feel before meditation?

What did you smell?

What did you hear?

What did you see?

Reflection.

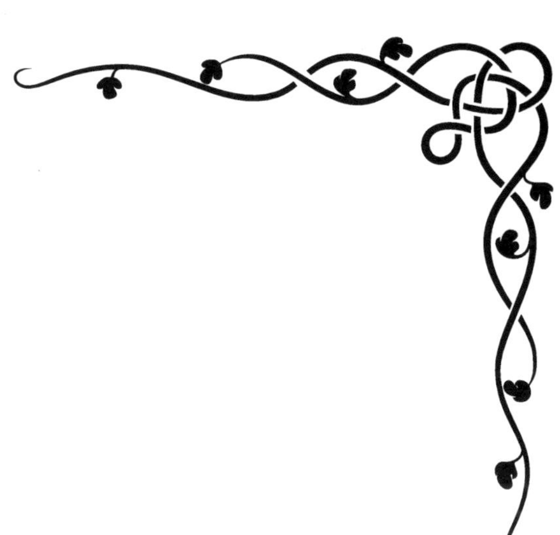

How do you feel now?

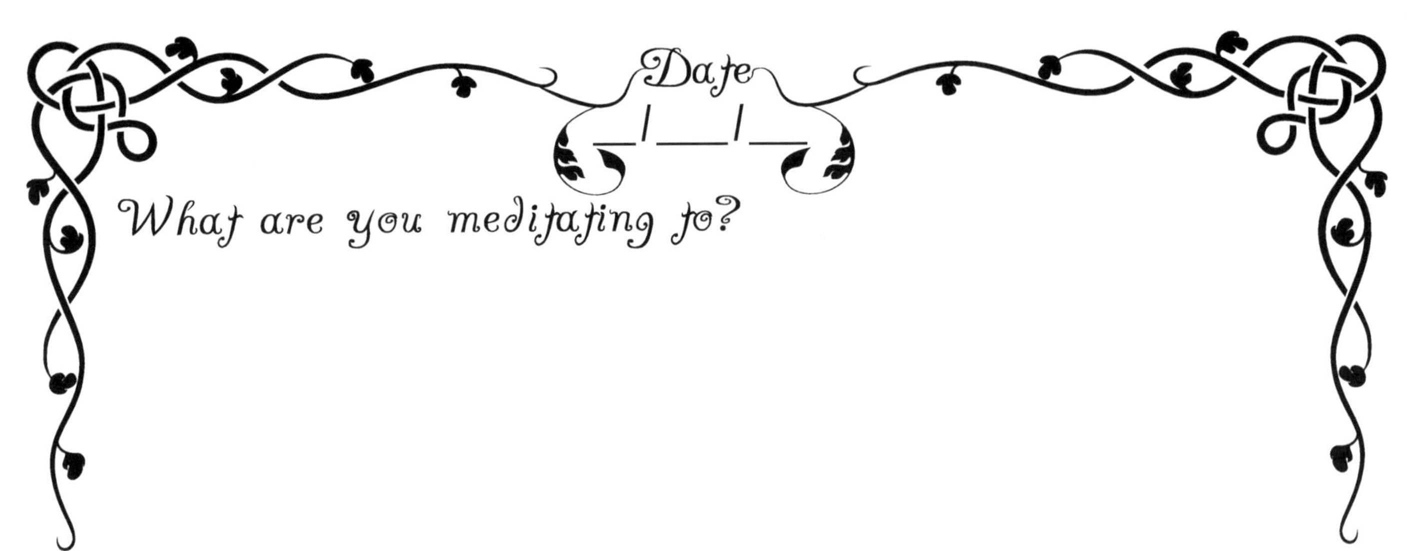

Date __/__/__

What are you meditating to?

How do you feel before meditation?

What did you smell?

What did you hear?

What did you see?

Reflection.

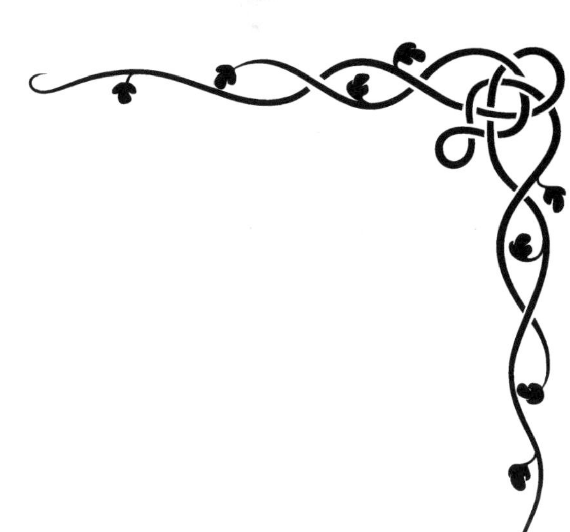

How do you feel now?

Date

__/__/__

What are you meditating to?

How do you feel before meditation?

What did you smell?

What did you hear?

What did you see?

Reflection.

How do you feel now?

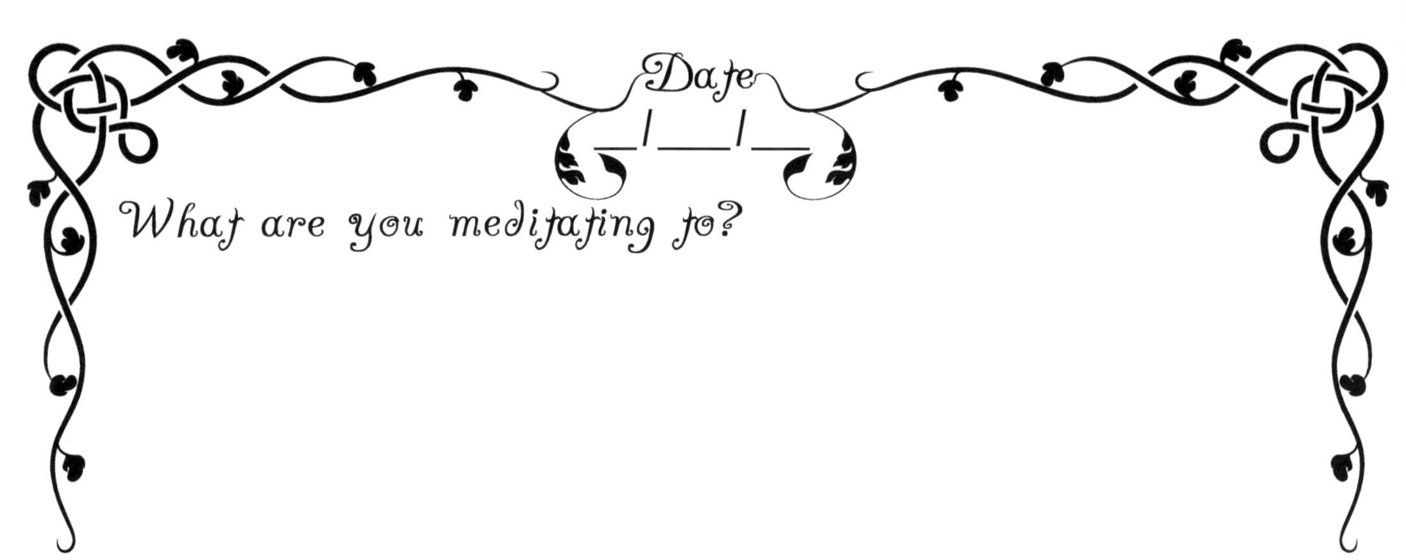

Date

__/__/__

What are you meditating to?

How do you feel before meditation?

What did you smell?

What did you hear?

What did you see?

Reflection.

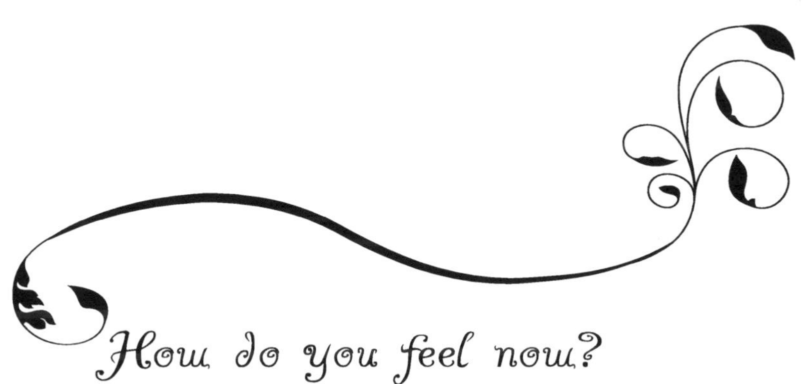

How do you feel now?

Meditation Playlist

Meditation Playlist

Notes

Notes

Suzi Spirit Sensitive

Suzi is a life coach, law of attraction practitioner, Tarot and Oracle card reader, writer for the International Paranormal Inquisitor and a spirit sensitive with P.P.I. She is also a mother of one and is based in the West of Ireland. Her goal is to motivate and inspire you to reach for your dreams and achieve your goals. She also seeks to bring you the best guidance from your Angel's, Ancestors, Guardians, Guides and loved ones in spirit. Suzi is best known for her straight talking nature and for her humour. She brings this into her work and people love her no-nonsense attitude. She is also a warm, kind hearted individual who seeks to empower people and to help them bring out the best in themselves. She has a number of platforms on social media including Facebook, Instagram and Twitter, however her biggest success is her YouTube channel in which she conducts pick a card readings, tutorials, reviews and mini lessons. She takes great pride in this as her online following grows everyday and she feels she is really getting her voice out there.

Printed in Poland
by Amazon Fulfillment
Poland Sp. z o.o., Wrocław

50680494R00114